FOOD
-&-
KINDNESS

THE SOBELL HOUSE
COOK BOOK

Colourful Punts on the River Cherwell, Oxford

"This book is dedicated to all our wonderful colleagues, volunteers and supporters, who help make Sobell House the very special place it is."

FOOD & KINDNESSS

THE SOBELL HOUSE COOK BOOK

©2020 Sobell House & Meze Publishing Ltd.
All rights reserved
First edition printed in 2020 in the UK
ISBN: 978-1-910863-70-1
Special thanks to: Mary Berry, Paul Chahidi, Stephen Fry, Mel Giedroyc & Sue Perkins
Written by: Katie Fisher
Compiled by: Tim Wraith, Lorraine Pink
Designed by: Phil Turner, Paul Cocker
Photography by: Paul Gregory
Additional Photos:
John Cairns. Madeleine Ball, Becca Wraith
Contributors: Michael Johnson,
Paul Stimpson, Esme Taylor, Emma Toogood

Published by Meze Publishing Limited
Unit 1b, 2 Kelham Square
Kelham Riverside
Sheffield S3 8SD
Web: www.mezepublishing.co.uk
Telephone: 0114 275 7709
Email: info@mezepublishing.co.uk

Sobell House
Churchill Hospital
Old Road
Headington
Oxford OX3 7LE
Web: www.sobellhouse.org
Telephone: 01865 857007
Email: mail@sobellhospice.org

Printed in Great Britain by Bell and Bain Ltd, Glasgow

Foreword

Food and Kindness is so much more than a cook book. It's a celebration of good food and those that make it, told through recipes and stories. As a well-known local charity, it's also an opportunity for us to show our support for the food and hospitality businesses in our area who have had such a tough time in 2020, many of whom have supported us over the years. What's more, thanks to the generosity of so many people, this book will be a fantastic fundraiser for Sobell House.

We are incredibly grateful to SMEG, I P Asset Partnership and Oxford Economics who have sponsored this book, meaning that all the money raised goes to the hospice. Places like Sobell House rely on the kindness and generosity of so many businesses and people and this is a great example of that. Thanks to Meze Publishing for producing the book.

I would also like to say thank you to our new Charity Ambassador, Paul Chahidi, who has become such a good friend to Sobell House. We have a recipe from Paul in the book and through his support are also able to include contributions from the wonderful Mary Berry, Mel Giedroyc, Sue Perkins and Stephen Fry.

Sobell House has touched the lives of people throughout Oxfordshire since 1976. Over the years we have cared for many people coming to the end of their lives, alongside their family and friends. As well as expert medical care, kindness and hospitality are absolutely at the core of life at the hospice and food is a huge part of that. That's why Sarah, our amazing chef, has also shared a recipe in this book. Food breaks down barriers, makes people feel relaxed and allows conversations to flow, even the difficult ones.

Sobell House is a place of great kindness and hospitality; both are central to so much of what goes on here. The word 'hospice' derives from hospitality, which is about welcoming other people into a home, or other places where we work and spend time. Everyone who comes to the hospice receives this welcome. Hospitality, food, kindness and care all come together here, making Sobell House the place it is today.

I hope you enjoy reading and cooking from this book as much as we have enjoyed putting it together. Sobell House is a very special place and in buying this book you are helping us to continue caring for and supporting local people now and in the future.

Diane Gardner   CEO Sobell House

Contents

Editorial

Foreword
by Chief Executive Sobell House Hospice Charity,
Diane Gardner   4

Introduction
Sobell House: a very special place   10

Directory   124

Guest Recipes

Mary Berry
Very Best Chocolate Cake   24

Mel Giedroyc
My Mum's Vegetable Soup   42

Paul Chahidi
Mediterranean Pork, Lemon
and Parmesan Meatballs   60

Stephen Fry
Bless Pots!   82

Sue Perkins
Jackfruit Wrap with Baba Ganoush   104

Recipes from friends of Sobell House

Sobell House
Meals that Matter   12
Mini Cheese & Onion and
Mini Brie & Tomato Quiches   14

Arbequina
A Little Bit of Alchemy   16
Beetroot Borani   18

Aziz
A Pioneering Approach   20
Machher Shaloon   22

Barefoot
More Than Just Cake   26
Carrot & Orange Cake   28

Bhoomi Kitchen
New Roots   30
Chicken 65   32

The Black Horse
Something Old, Something New   34
Tandoori Spiced Lamb with Samosa,
Dhal and Chutneys   36

The Butchers Arms
Fit as a Butcher's Dog   38
Beetroot and Mint Burgers   40

The Cherwell Boathouse
Take a Punt on the Boathouse   44
Breaded Halloumi, Avocado,
Sweetcorn Fritter, Lime   46

Christine Bakes

Life Is What You Bake It 48

Summer Fruit Roll with
Lemon Mascarpone Cream 50

Cuttlefish

The Perfect Catch 52

Mediterranean Fish Soup 54

Jolly Good Brownies

Home Sweet Home 56

Raw Chocolate Orange Fruit and Nut Bars 58

La Cucina

A Little Slice of Italy 62

Risotto Milanese con Osso Bucco 64

Lotte Duncan

A Recipe for Success 66

Lemon and Basil Pasta 68

The Mole Inn

Holy Moley! 70

Tuna Tartare with Avocado Purée
and Black Garlic Mayo 72

Natural Bread

Rising to the Occasion 74

Financiers 76

No.1 Ship Street

Pushing the Boat Out 78

French Onion Soup 80

Nut Tree Inn

Sticking to your Roots 84

Pig's Head & Black Pudding Terrine
with Piccalilli 86

Oli's Thai

Life of Thai 88

Aubergine Curry 90

Oxford Fine Dining

A Moveable Feast 92

Chicken Breast, Pea Purée
and Wild Garlic Hollandaise 94

Pindy's Samosas

Spiced, Sealed, Delivered 96

Chickpea and Red Pepper Curry 98

The Secret Supper Society

Be Our Guest 100

Crab Linguine 102

SMEG

Buon Appetito! 106

Pizza 108

Pumpkin Risotto 110

White Chocolate & Ricotta Mousse
with Blueberry Sauce 112

White Hart Fyfield

Passionate about Provenance 114

Elderflower Crème Brûlée
with Gooseberry Compote 116

The White Hart at Wytham

The Hart of the Village 118

Iced Banana Parfait with Salted Caramel 120

Radcliffe Camera and All Souls College, Oxford University, Oxford

Sobell House: a very special place

Sobell House, based in Oxford, is one of the oldest hospices in the UK and is jointly funded by the NHS and Sobell House Hospice Charity. Since 1976 it has been caring for adults with life-limiting illnesses and providing support to their families. At any one time, we are caring for approximately 500 patients across Oxfordshire. We believe that every adult should be able to die with dignity and without pain.

The charity provides approximately 30% of the hospice running costs, working with the NHS clinical teams to ensure that the charitable funding enhances and complements the highly skilled and compassionate care that they give to patients. This is done through the provision of funds to develop service projects in addition to the 'extras' that make people's experiences at Sobell House so special. These include our art and music therapies, bereavement support, and the very popular drinks trolley that goes around every day so patients can enjoy their favourite tipple!

The care and support provided by Sobell House is delivered at our purpose-built hospice, containing a Day Centre and Inpatient Unit, as well as in people's homes and Oxfordshire hospitals. Our aim is to support people to live as well and as fully as they can in the time they have left. Far from being a dark and unhappy place, our hospice is full of light and joy. Yes, there is sadness but there is also much love and laughter. Everyone who comes to the hospice is touched by the care and compassion provided by staff. Here are two examples of the difference our dedicated team make in the lives of those we care for:

"If it wasn't for Sobell House, I'm not sure how I could have ever coped. They are the most lovely, selfless people who make the lives of others a priority, working long, hard hours but always maintaining a high standard of care and love. I will always be forever grateful to everyone at Sobell and hope this great place will continue to care for many years to come." *Yasmine's experience of the care we provided to her mother, Gina*

"Tom, the music therapist, was an inspiration to me. I had written a song when I was 19 about an imaginary lost love: 'Gorgeous Girl'. I had written some extra words for Anny and for quite a while I had secretly planned to sing it at Anny's funeral. I asked Tom if he would help me record it with a bit of extra accompaniment to go with my guitar. He was brilliant – I sang it through and he added a much richer backing. It was a difficult moment when I told Anny I wanted to play the song at her funeral, but it meant so much to be able to play the CD to Anny in her room. We were both very emotional and crying our eyes out, but it was very rewarding as music is such a powerful way to express those deep thoughts of love and loss." *Peter talking about the care we provided to his wife Anny*

Sobell House is a very special place where kindness and care are central to everything we do.

Meals that Matter

Food and friendship are central to everything Sobell House is about; we recognise that for many people, what they eat and drink is as important as medicine.

Eating and drinking are a big part of everyday life for most people. As well as providing us with nutrition, food offers comfort and can evoke memories and emotions. As a hospice providing specialist palliative care, we appreciate the importance of this, but are also acutely aware that for many of our patients there can also be a reduction in appetite due to their illness.

That's why at Sobell House we cater to individual needs. From breakfasts to hot lunches, evening meals to light suppers, nothing is mass-produced. As you can imagine, this requires plenty of flexibility and the ability at times to think outside the box. Here at Sobell House, we are very fortunate to have a resident chef, Sarah Overton, who has been committed to doing this for over twelve years in her time working at the hospice:

"My job can be both very rewarding and very challenging at times; every day is so different. Some patients have special diets and other patients need specific food items. We don't like saying no, so we try to accommodate all our patient needs and wants. I love what I do here."

There's more to food and friendship here than everyday meals, though. Sarah has also catered for events, such as last-minute patient weddings at the hospice, enabling couples to celebrate their special day together, surrounded by friends and family. There's even a drinks trolley brought round every evening so people can enjoy a glass of wine with dinner or have their favourite tipple! This is hugely popular and is always remembered fondly by friends and family.

The food Sarah creates is neither flamboyant nor institutional; she aims for wholesome and nutritious meals that are homely and 'normal' to make Sobell House a home-from-home. On the first Monday of every month the staff look forward to Sarah's homemade cakes at their Team Meeting, which are often inspired by recipes from Mary Berry, of whom she is a great fan.

For some, it's not just about eating food, but the preparation. We enabled one of our patients to relive happy memories of baking at home by making a cake with his brother in our Day Centre kitchen and tucking into a slice in bed! This understanding of why food is important is integral to the care we provide at the hospice. As with any service that supports people at the end of their lives, Sobell House strives to make every moment matter.

Mini Cheese & Onion and Mini Brie & Tomato Quiches

Sarah provides food for members of staff as well as patients. Her mini quiches are legendary and enjoyed by everyone! They look wonderful too and only take about an hour to prepare.

Preparation time: 45-50 minutes | Cooking time: 12-15 minutes | Makes 24 mini quiches

For the shortcrust pastry
250g plain flour
130g butter or margarine
3-4 tbsp cold water
For the fillings
1 medium-sized tomato
3-4 spring onions

2 eggs
250ml whole milk
Salt and pepper
100g mature cheddar cheese, grated
A wedge of brie (150-200g)

For the shortcrust pastry

Rub the butter or margarine into the flour until it resembles fine breadcrumbs, add the water gradually and mix to form a soft dough. Wrap the pastry in cling film and place in the fridge to rest for 30 minutes. Meanwhile, prepare the fillings and grease two 12-hole bun tins.

For the fillings

Deseed and finely dice the tomato, finely slice the spring onions, beat the eggs and milk together in a jug then season with salt and pepper.

Roll out the chilled pastry and press out 24 circles using a round cutter, in a size that will line the holes in the bun tins. Gently press the pastry rounds into the tins so you have 24 cases.

Divide the diced tomato between 12 of the pastry cases. Divide the spring onions between the other 12 pastry cases, then sprinkle the grated cheddar cheese on top of the spring onions. Thinly slice the brie and place it on top of the tomatoes, dividing evenly between the cases.

Gently pour the egg and milk mixture into each mini quiche so it covers the fillings but doesn't overflow. Bake them in the oven for 12 to 15 minutes at 180°c. Serve warm or leave to cool.

A Little Bit of Alchemy

Named after a type of olive oil that garnishes many tapas dishes with its signature flavour, Arbequina brings the best of Spanish food, drink and atmosphere to Oxford with as much individuality as its namesake.

Arbequina opened its doors in 2016, but the story of this vibrant tapas restaurant is intertwined with a building that has more than a century of history. Ben Whyles owns the venue, which he ran as a restaurant for twelve years before taking the plunge with a couple of old friends: Rufus (who also co-owns Oli's Thai) and Ben, who became Arbequina's general manager, to make their shared dream a reality.

They closed the former restaurant, gutted it completely and redesigned the space over three months, doing much of the work themselves.

As they scraped off layers of paint on the shop front, decades fell away to reveal carved wooden signage with gold paint inlaid, reading R.A. Neville Dispensing Chemist.

Their landlord's surname was Neville, and turned out to be the grandson of the shop's original owner who established his venture back in the very early 1900s. Keeping this piece of Oxford's social history alive, the trio decided to re-glaze the sign and use the hundred year old glass as part of the decor inside.

That attention to detail demonstrates how invested the three founders — Ben, Rufus and Ben — are in their own venture, and this dedication is strongly reflected in the food, drink and atmosphere of Arbequina.

"Tapas style food for sharing, with explosive flavours that marry well together, is something we all felt passionate about," explains general manager Ben. Quality comes first, whether they're sourcing from local suppliers or Spanish producers who marinate their own olives.

The bar is a focal point in the small restaurant, allowing diners to watch the chefs and bartenders preparing their orders and creating the fun, vibrant atmosphere that makes each visit not just a meal but a real event.

To complement the Spanish menu, a large section of the drinks offering is sherry, often unfairly maligned as the stuff of grandparents' cabinets in Britain, but a wonderful match for many tapas flavours. Ben also curates a collection of organic and natural wines, and since its first week of being exported to the UK, Arbequina has served the Spanish draught beer Palax, more recently joined by ales brewed much closer to home, from Tap Social in Oxford.

In 2019, the team opened a cocktail bar in the formerly derelict venue next door, which they have since been able to incorporate, creating a bigger space for guests to relax with a drink, share food, and soak up the unique atmosphere.

Arbequina

R. A. NEVILLE.
Dispensing Chemist.

SHERRY & BRANDY

Beetroot Borani

Although borani is a traditionally Iranian appetiser, the flavours work in perfect harmony with Spanish and Mediterranean food. Our Beetroot Borani has been a staple on our menu since we first opened and continues to be one of our best-selling dishes! It's best served as a dip with fresh bread.

Preparation time: 30 minutes | Cooking time: 1 hour | Serves: 6

For the borani
1kg red beetroot
60ml extra-virgin olive oil
30ml balsamic vinegar (we use Pedro Ximenez)
1 tbsp yoghurt
1 clove of garlic

3 sprigs of fresh dill
Salt
For the garnish
1 yellow beetroot
1-2 sprigs of fresh dill
25ml Moscatel dessert wine (or another sweet wine)

50g feta cheese
4-5 walnuts, broken into pieces

Peel and chop the red beetroot into discs 1cm thick. Mix them in a roasting tray with 20ml of water, 10ml of the olive oil and 10ml of the vinegar. Cover with tin foil and roast for 1 hour, or until soft. For the last 15 minutes of the roasting time, remove the tin foil to allow the beetroot to slightly caramelise, as this adds a lot of flavour! Remove from the oven and leave to cool.

Add the roasted beetroot, remaining olive oil and vinegar, yoghurt, garlic and dill to a blender. Blend the ingredients into a rough purée and season the mixture with salt to taste. You now have the Beetroot Borani base, which can be kept for up to 72 hours in the fridge.

Peel and very finely dice the yellow beetroot. Finely chop the dill then stir it into the diced beetroot along with the sweet wine. This can also be kept for up to 72 hours in the fridge, stored separately to the red beetroot base. Drain thoroughly before using.

To serve

Spread the base into a bowl or other serving dish. Arrange the soaked yellow beetroot in a pile in the centre of your borani. Crumble the feta and walnut pieces around the dish and tear some more dill over the top. Drizzle with a dash of olive oil and the dish is ready to serve with fresh bread or crispbread on the side for dipping.

A Pioneering Approach

Fusing Indian and Bangladeshi cuisines, Aziz Restaurant is a well-established destination in Oxfordshire with a deserved reputation for innovative, creative and delicious food.

Aziz Rahman opened his first eponymous restaurant in 1990 with the aim of showcasing Bangladeshi cuisine. The restaurateur is from Syhlet in Bangladesh. He moved to Oxford with his family in 1969 and began his involvement with the restaurant trade in 1978 which led to several successful ventures across the county.

Creating Aziz Restaurant meant that he could combine Western influences with the food that he had grown up with, which wasn't often recognised in Britain as separate from 'Indian' cuisine, itself very regional and nuanced.

Inspired by chefs he had worked with and his interest in picking up new ideas when discovering restaurants, Aziz brought in head chef Nurul Amin who took the restaurant's food to the next level. They then brought in a completely new menu during summer 2020, designed to recreate a very authentic way of eating Indian food for the first time in the restaurant's history. Customers can tick items on the menu to customise their thali, a platter that might include various curries, dahls, rice, naans and other accompaniments to enjoy as one meal.

Aziz Restaurant also offers online ordering for takeaways, and has a catering arm that comprises full service and event management with traditional or tailored menus for any occasion.

During its 30 years, there have been several branches of Aziz Restaurant across Oxfordshire, and the most recent of these opened in The Tree Hotel in 2019. Customers have visited from all over the world; the staff find that tourists often have the restaurant earmarked to dine at thanks to its far-reaching reputation, and have also welcomed many celebrities and dignitaries over the years.

The restaurant's accolades include British Curry Awards, recommendations in the Hardens Guide, mentions in the Observer and Sunday Times as well as local recognition from the Oxford Mail, in which Chris Gray described Aziz as "the institute of curry restaurants."

As chairman of the Dine Bangladeshi Campaign (which was created to raise awareness that most Indian restaurants in the UK are actually Bangladeshi) and founding chairman of the Guild of Bangladeshi Restaurateurs Association, it's fair to say that Aziz Rahman has led the way for innovation and creativity in Bangladeshi and Indian cuisine across Oxfordshire.

His restaurant's local, national and international recognition is testament to the unique approach he pioneered in centering Bangladeshi food for Oxfordshire and beyond to discover.

Machher Shaloon

This fish curry uses aromatic spices to give your choice of fillets a delicately balanced yet exciting flavour.

Preparation time: 5 minutes | Cooking time: 25-30 minutes | Serves: 4-6

500g fish of your choice, portioned into 5cm pieces
3 tbsp oil
½ a cup of sliced onions
1 tsp finely chopped garlic
½ tsp grated ginger
1 tsp turmeric

½ tsp cayenne pepper
½ tsp ground coriander
½ tsp ground cumin
Salt, according to your taste
1 cup of water, or as needed
3 green chillies
Handful of fresh coriander, chopped

Heat the oil in a medium-sized pan and fry the sliced onions over a medium heat until just turning lightly golden. Add the garlic, ginger, turmeric, cayenne, coriander, cumin and salt. Stir and fry for a few minutes.

Place fish into the pan in a single layer and fry with the spices for several minutes, gently turning the pieces over once.

Add the water and chillies. Cover the pan and cook on a medium heat for 10 to 15 minutes or until the fish is cooked through. Add more water, up to another half a cup, if needed.

Garnish the curry with the fresh coriander and serve it with basmati rice or flatbreads.

Mary Berry's
Very Best Chocolate Cake

Who doesn't love a chocolate cake? This is a real crowd pleaser that the whole family will love. For many years I have been making this recipe for my children, and now my grandchildren. Weigh carefully and use the right size tin and oven temperature, and it will be just lovely.

Preparation time: 10 minutes, plus 10 minutes cooling | Cooking time: 25-30 minutes | Serves: 6-8

50g cocoa powder
6 tbsp boiling water
3 eggs
4 tbsp milk
175g self-raising flour
1 level tsp baking powder
100g baking spread or soft butter

300g natural caster sugar

For the icing and filling

150g Bournville chocolate, broken into small pieces
150ml pouring double cream
3 tbsp apricot jam

Preheat the oven to 180°c or 160°c fan. Grease two 20cm sandwich tins and line the base with baking parchment.

First, measure the cocoa and boiling water into a large bowl then mix well to make a paste. Add the remaining ingredients for the cake and beat again until combined. This can also be made in a processor but be careful not to over mix. Divide the cake mixture between the prepared tins.

Bake in the preheated oven for about 25 to 30 minutes until well risen, shrinking away from the sides of the tin and springy to the touch.

For the icing and filling

Measure the chocolate and cream into a bowl and stand the bowl over a pan of simmering water for about 10 minutes until melted, stirring from time to time. Set aside and allow the mixture to become cold and almost set.

When baked, leave the cakes for 10 minutes to cool a little. Carefully transfer them from the tin to a wire rack and allow to cool completely. Spread the tops of each cake with apricot jam. Fill the cakes with half the icing and spread the remainder on top. Take a small palette knife and make a pretty swirl pattern on top, then dust with icing sugar and enjoy!

More Than Just Cake

Barefoot is a bakery, coffee shop and cake lovers' heaven in Oxford. It was established by self-confessed foodie Emily, who built her business from the ground up with hard work, determination, and really good cake!

Emily had always been a home baker alongside her work in wedding planning, event organisation and catering. While shopping at farmers' markets and exploring London's food scene, Emily found much to admire in the local producers and their products, so she decided to join the party by setting up her own small business.

She and her husband Fraser are real foodies who love eating out, discovering new places, researching recipes, entertaining and shopping for fresh local ingredients, so it was a combination of valuable experience and a passion for food that paved the way for her venture to flourish.

Emily and Fraser returned to Oxford in 2013; Fraser was working for Jamie Oliver and Emily found a gap in the market for a cake stall which would feature all her signature cakes, salted caramel brownies and banana bread. Despite sharing a small kitchen with Fraser's parents, with whom they moved in at first, Emily began baking in earnest with her trusty KitchenAid. Her first pitch was at North Parade Market and, having prepared until 3am then fought back fears about how it would all be received, the day was a complete success and Barefoot was born! The stall sold out and Emily not only received amazing feedback from customers but orders too, and cafés asking for her cakes.

Barefoot continued to sell out every market day and gained regulars alongside a wider interest in the bakes. The trade supply list grew and grew, and for the next two years Emily hired ovens, baked through the night, packed, invoiced and delivered to keep up with demand. A very sad turn of events led to her father passing away in Florida, and at the same time she was offered a lease on a perfect shop in the most perfect location, so Emily had to make the snap decision of whether to take it on.

"I can still remember the exact moment when I said okay, let's go for it," she says. Since then, she hasn't looked back and the shop has gone from strength to strength.

"We have the most wonderful team of bakers and shop staff who make it all work," she continues. "Barefoot has become a family for customers and staff. It's more than just cake; it feels like home." Although Emily hadn't planned to expand so much, Barefoot has grown organically to fulfil its founder's ambitions of making people happy by baking, and has become a much-loved part of the foodie scene in Oxford.

CAKE

COFFEE

PASTRIES

SWEET LUNCH

WIFI

TAKE OUT

PRIVATE ORDERS

74^A

CAKE

Carrot & Orange Cake

This recipe makes one 25cm (10 inch) double layer cake and serves twelve people with giant portions! It should be kept in the fridge but removed an hour before serving, and eaten within seven days.

Preparation time: 20 minutes | Cooking time: 45-55 minutes | Serves: 12 (giant portions)

For the cream cheese frosting	300g caster sugar	100g dried dates, chopped
125g salted butter	300g dark brown sugar	100g clementines, peeled
800g full fat cream cheese	1 tsp vanilla extract	600g self-raising flour
125g icing sugar	1 tsp salt	150g walnuts, crushed
2 tsp vanilla extract	6 free-range eggs	**For the decoration**
For the cake	2 tsp ground cinnamon and nutmeg	75g walnuts, crushed
525g light olive oil	300g carrot, grated	1 large orange

For the cream cheese frosting

Melt the butter slowly in the microwave or a pan until there are no solids left. Add the liquid butter to a bowl or mixer with half the cream cheese and mix until completely combined, then add the rest of the cream cheese and mix again. Add the vanilla then sift in the icing sugar. Mix for about 1 minute or until smooth, then place the frosting in the fridge until you need it.

For the cake

Grease and line two 25cm (10 inch) round cake tins. Preheat the oven to 150°c. Weigh out all the ingredients; this will save time and help you avoid going wrong. Boil a kettle, cover the chopped dates with boiling water and leave to one side. Blend the peeled clementines to a fairly smooth purée.

Place the oil, sugars, vanilla, salt and eggs in a mixing bowl. Combine with a stand mixer or electric handheld whisk, or beat by hand with a whisk for about 2 minutes, until light and fluffy and fully combined. Add the cinnamon, nutmeg and grated carrot, and mix for about 30 seconds, or until combined. Add the dates, including the liquid they were steeping in, and the blitzed clementines. Mix for a further 1 to 2 minutes, until totally combined. Add all the flour and chopped walnuts, then mix until the flour is fully incorporated which should only take about 30 seconds. Using a spatula, scrape around the bowl, and right to the bottom, to ensure all the flour is combined. Do not over mix the batter once the flour has been added, otherwise your cake will be tough.

Split the mixture between your two tins then pop them into the preheated oven. Cook for 45 to 55 minutes, or when a cocktail stick or skewer comes out clean.

For the decoration

Once the cakes have completely cooled in their tins, turn them out. Place one layer on a cake board, stand, or plate. Frost the first layer, then sprinkle the top with crushed walnuts and finely grate over some orange zest. Carefully place the next layer on top and repeat the process, using plenty of orange zest for garnish on the top.

Store the finished cake in the fridge (because of the cream cheese frosting) for up to 7 days, and remove 1 hour before eating.

New Roots

Bringing the food of southern India to southern England, the reimagined Bhoomi Kitchen is a place of authenticity and innovation, with branches in Cheltenham and Oxford.

The story of Bhoomi Kitchen begins not in Cheltenham, where the restaurant first opened, but in a southern Indian village where a farmer first discovered his love for cooking.

Appacha moved to the UK in the 1960s to live with a family in Burford as their chef, and later settled in Cheltenham. His strong connection to the area, the recipes he brought from Kerala and his passion for food inspired Michael, Appacha's grandson, to establish a restaurant that celebrated southern Indian cuisine.

From 2013 to 2019, Bhoomi offered tasting menus and fine dining with a difference.

"It was a process of evolving and learning, but I'm a person who doesn't like to sit still: I love food and coming up with new ideas, so when it felt like the right time for us and our customers, I started planning a relaunch of the business," Michael explains.

After working on the format, developing menus and securing a second venue, he opened Bhoomi Kitchen in Cheltenham, with an Oxford branch following in 2020. The concept quickly caught on thanks to the casual but high end vibe, upbeat atmosphere and vibrant food.

The new, more relaxed restaurants allow diners to mix and match between sections of the menu. There are classic dishes such as traditional Keralan curries, thali for speedy but delicious pre-theatre meals, small plates for sharing and Indian barbecue, all freshly prepared by specialist chefs. It was important for these parts of southern Indian culture to be expressed with such flexible food, alongside a fun selection of Indian-inspired cocktails and plenty of beer or lassi to complement the charcoal-grilled meats and vegetarian or vegan dishes.

Bhoomi Kitchen also serves an unusual pork tenderloin curry alongside the beef and lamb specials, showcasing a wide range of southern Indian cuisine which is often less represented here.

Despite coming from a background in retail, Michael's forward-thinking approach coupled with a genuine love of food, including his own culinary heritage, has led to great success as a restaurateur. Having made a life-changing move into something he'd always wanted to do, he found a balance between family and business that allows Bhoomi Kitchen to flourish.

Since then, it has been listed in the Michelin Guide and Harden's Guide, won the Taste of Gloucestershire Award in 2016 and was recently named Best Restaurant in the South West by the Asian Curry Awards.

Chicken 65

Our recipe is for South Indian style fried chicken. Spice rubbed, fried and best served with tangy mango raita. A true South Indian staple.

Preparation time: 30 minutes | Cooking time: 10 minutes | Serves: 6-8

1 tbsp Kashmiri chilli powder
1 tbsp ground coriander
1 tbsp ground cumin
1 tbsp garam masala
½ tbsp haldi powder (turmeric)
½ tbsp cornflour
½ tbsp fine rice flour

¾ tbsp garlic paste
1 tbsp lemon juice
1 tbsp curry leaves, finely chopped
2 tbsp coriander leaves, finely chopped
2 tbsp vegetable oil
Pinch of salt, to taste

1kg chicken breast, cut into cubes
500ml vegetable oil, for frying

Mix all the ingredients except the chicken breast and vegetable oil for frying together, stirring until they form a paste. Add the chicken to the spice paste and mix well for 2 minutes. Leave the chicken to marinate for half an hour.

Pour the vegetable oil into a deep frying pan on a high heat. Once the oil is hot, turn down to a medium heat and add the marinated chicken one piece at a time. Cook the chicken for around 8 minutes or until thoroughly cooked through, then serve straightaway.

Something Old, Something New

The Black Horse in Standlake has very quickly gained a reputation for excellent food and an experience that sets it apart from the average village pub, drawing locals and visitors to a dining destination that's newly back on the map.

Nick Evans grew up in Standlake and, despite having escaped London for sunny Spain and retirement, was keen to return and give the old village pub an exciting new lease of life. The Black Horse was taken over by his team in November 2019 and rose to local fame within just a few months.

"We want customers to think 'wow, what an experience for a village pub' and for The Black Horse to become bigger than what it was, embracing the locals, who have now found a place to enjoy great food, wine or simply a pint after work," explains Nick, the owner, and his son Sebastian, the front of house manager. "It was a bit unloved, and hopefully we've put a fair bit of love back in."

The pub's transformation is due in no small part to the food created by executive head chef Martin Sheriff, who is classically French trained but known for his contemporary style that adds flair and depth of flavour to every dish. He deliberately sources ingredients from very local suppliers to ensure the produce is top quality, and recognises the importance of visual impact. The exciting seasonal menus, not to mention hundreds of positive online reviews, are sure to entice you to try any one of its carefully comprised dishes.

The Black Horse has an extensive selection of bottled beers and lagers, cocktails and spirits, plus a handpicked wine list that showcases Nick's passion for quality from the rare to the classic. Whether you're looking for somewhere to sip your favourite tipple or enjoy a delicious meal out, the pub offers plenty of options come rain or shine. The large garden has lots of picnic benches, and the undercover patio creates an almost Mediterranean feel with a wood-burning pizza oven and huge pans of seafood paella to eat al fresco.

Indoors, you'll find open fires, exposed beams, cosy seating and the really friendly welcome that only an authentic village local can offer. The Black Horse was a finalist in the 2020 Ox In A Box Awards for Best Gastropub, demonstrating how much hard work and genuine care has gone into the project over just the first few months. From live music to wine tastings and pints in the sunshine to memorable meals, there's more to this little piece of old England than first meets the eye, and its vibrant atmosphere makes it the place to be any day of the week.

Tandoori Spiced Lamb with Samosa, Dhal and Chutneys

This dish embraces Indian cooking while adding modern flair, staying true to traditional flavours that remind you of your favourite curry house. This dish has it all: chutneys, samosa, dhal and delicious tandoori spiced lamb.

Preparation time: 15-20 minutes | Cooking time: 15-20 minutes | Serves: 2

For the tandoori lamb
2 x 180g pieces of lamb rump
A spoonful of tandoori spices
For the red lentil dhal
1 shallot & garlic clove, finely chopped
1 tomato, finely chopped
1 tsp madras curry powder
½ tsp smoked paprika

2 tbsp vegetable oil
100g red split lentils
For the minced lamb samosa
100g minced lamb
1 shallot, finely chopped
20g frozen peas
2 tbsp madras curry powder
2 tbsp lemon juice

1 pack of spring roll pastry
1 tbsp flour
For the prune & tamarind purée
100g prunes
1 tbsp tamarind paste
For the buttermilk dip
100g buttermilk
4 tbsp finely chopped fresh mint

For the tandoori lamb

Roll the pieces of lamb rump in the tandoori spices. Pan fry the lamb briefly in a little oil to lock in all the flavours. Finally, place in the oven for 12 minutes at 180°c to cook the lamb rare (it will be pink in the middle) or leave it for 15 minutes for medium. Rest briefly before serving.

For the red lentil dhal

Fry the shallot, garlic and tomato together with the spices in the vegetable oil. Once softened, add the red lentils and cook the dhal like a risotto, adding water as you go and making sure you do not let it dry out. When done, the lentils should be tender and the dhal should be fairly thick.

For the minced lamb samosa

Place the minced lamb, shallot, frozen peas, curry powder and lemon juice into a frying pan and gently cook until the meat has browned. Leave the filling to cool, then lay out a sheet of the spring roll pastry and spoon the lamb mixture onto it. Fold the edges in to form a parcel (it doesn't have to be triangular) and mix the flour with some water to form a paste to glue them together. Heat a thin layer of oil in a clean frying pan and shallow fry the samosa until the pastry is golden.

For the prune and tamarind purée

Place the prunes and paste in a saucepan with 300ml of water, then gently poach over a low heat until smooth. Whizz to a purée in a blender.

For the buttermilk dip

Simply blend the ingredients together, then transfer into a small bowl. Serve the hot tandoori lamb with the samosa and purée on a warm plate, alongside the red lentil dhal and buttermilk dip in bowls.

Fit as a Butcher's Dog

The Butchers Arms has been around for over 150 years, so Paul and Pippa Hitchcock want to keep that legacy alive while bringing their own personalities to the Headington local.

Having reached a point where they wanted a change from professional jobs that didn't leave them much time together, Paul and Pippa Hitchcock were looking at options for running a pub when they spotted a favourite local of theirs, The Butchers Arms, was looking for new landlords. They knew the pub business was right for them because "you can't fake being interested in people," and they had found interaction the most rewarding part of previous jobs. Within a few weeks they were in!

Over the following years Paul and Pippa built the pub up from a small business to a busy and vibrant pillar of the community with a small tight-knit team, full of good ideas and determination. The Butchers Arms has had write ups in The Good Pub Guide, great customer feedback, and more recently a spot in CAMRA's Good Beer Guide two years running, putting it amongst Oxford's top watering holes.

"It's been a rollercoaster but an amazing ride," say the couple, "and we've been incredibly lucky with the community here; you can't guarantee that you'll fall into a place and it feels like home."

As a Fullers establishment, the pub is led by its fantastic selection of ales alongside a wide selection of gins, whiskeys and wines curated by Pippa. Paul takes charge of the cellar, making sure everything is tip top condition.

"We take a lot of pride in trying new things. Fullers give us free rein to choose from a huge range of cask and craft ales, so we can keep all of our regulars' favourites and experiment with some more unusual options."

The informal surroundings complement the menu of proper pub classics as well as pizzas and burgers, including many veggie and vegan options. People come back for the pies or beer battered fish and chips, and there's always something new to try on the weekly specials board. Paul and Pippa never compromise on quality, believing that care and attention makes all the difference when it comes to enjoying a good meal out as a family.

They also welcome four-legged friends, having five of their own (though Geri the cat isn't quite as dog friendly!) and enjoy getting to know their canine customers alongside the locals. Weekly quizzes and regular fundraising events also provide an opportunity to support their community, which is at the heart of everything Paul and Pippa aim to do here.

THE BUTCHERS ARMS

DEUS · NOBIS · OMNIA DAT

FULLER'S
Independent
FAMILY
BREWERS
Since 1845

LONDON
PRIDE

BEER
GARDEN

(CLOSES 11PM)

Beetroot and Mint Burgers

At The Butchers Arms we love great fresh ingredients and serve wholesome, filling meals the whole family will love. One of our favourites is our beetroot and mint burger, a simple but tasty vegetarian treat.

Preparation time: 60 minutes, plus 2 hours refrigerating | Cooking time: 10 minutes | Serves: 5

100g millet seeds
175ml lightly salted water
150g raw beetroot, grated
175g courgette, grated
30g carrots, grated
20g mint, finely chopped
20ml cider vinegar

20ml extra-virgin olive oil, plus extra for frying
35g cornflour
1 egg
225ml natural yoghurt
10g garlic, finely chopped
Salt and pepper

To serve
5 multi-grain buns, split
Lettuce leaves
Sliced beef tomato
Sliced pickled gherkins for garnish

Rinse and drain the millet and place into a small saucepan with the salted water. Place over a medium heat, bring to a simmer, cover and cook over a very low heat for 20 to 25 minutes until tender. Remove from the heat and leave to stand for 5 minutes, covered.

Put the beetroot, courgette, carrots and mint into a large bowl. Add the millet, vinegar, oil, a pinch of salt and pepper then mix well. Add the cornflour and egg and mix again, then chill in the refrigerator for 2 hours.

Put the yoghurt in a fine strainer over a bowl and drain for at least 40 minutes. Stir in the garlic and season to taste with salt and pepper.

Pack the beetroot mixture into a 125ml cup, then turn out and shape into a patty. Repeat to make five burgers. Place a ridged griddle pan or large frying pan over a medium heat and coat with oil. Add the patties and cook for approximately 5 minutes on each side, turning carefully, until brown.

To serve

Spread the buns with the yoghurt sauce and place the burgers in the buns, topped with lettuce, a slice of beef tomato, and sliced pickled gherkin. Serve immediately.

Mel Giedroyc's
My Mum's Vegetable Soup

This is one of those recipes that's been handed down through the generations. I think that my mum's grandmother in Portugal bequeathed it to my grandmother, who passed it down to my mum, on to me, and I've drilled my two daughters so they know it by heart now. They've been brought up on this soup, as have I.

My mum was a volunteer gardener at Sobell House in the 80s and I remember kneeling down beside her in the beds and helping her weed. It's a good leveller, weeding. And this soup is great after an outdoorsy activity like gardening. It's the sort of soup to have when you're feeling wobbly or low, too. It's a spirit perker-upper.

I hope you don't mind the slight vagueness when it comes to exact weights and measures. My mum's not that kind of person. She'll use terms like "smallish handful", "almost a spoonful", "a smidgin", "a whiff" or "the tiniest squidge". Don't worry, you can make it your own. I'm just going to set out the basics... oh and by the way, for some reason this soup ALWAYS tastes better the next day. Who knows why? But it does!

Preparation time: 10 minutes | Serves: 2-4

1 medium-size potato	Bouillon or vegetable stock	Mushroom ketchup, if you're feeling
The same weight of carrot (to match the potato)	Handful of chopped cabbage (the crunchy stuff works best I reckon)	frisky
1 clove of garlic	Handful of chopped celery	Lea & Perrins
Olive oil	Handful of chopped cauliflower florets	Kucharek (magic Polish granules, fabulous for any soup making activity)
1 tin of chopped tomatoes, a few fresh tomatoes, or both	1 bouquet garni	Vigorous amounts of black pepper
	1 bay leaf	Salt, to season

Chop the potato and carrot into cubes then crush the clove of garlic. Sweat all three in olive oil (a tablespoon-ish should be enough) in a solid pan on a medium heat with the lid on. You'll probably need to do this for about two songs worth of Gary Numan. When they're good and sweaty (as you'll be if you've been dancing along to the Gary Numan songs), add the tin of chopped tomatoes, fresh tomatoes or both and then bring to a rolling boil with about a litre of boiling bouillon (or veg stock made from a stock cube).

Throw in your cabbage, celery and cauliflower and let it roll, while adding the bouquet garni and bay leaf. Splash in a tablespoon-ish of mushroom ketchup and a good shake of Lea & Perrins. Bring the soup down to a simmer. Taste after about 15 minutes. If you need to call on your Polish friend Kucharek at this point, do so. If it's not available, don't worry, a bit of salt might do the trick. Grind some pepper in and assess the soup. If it looks a bit lumpy and bumpy you might want to add more bouillon. Do so. This is not a pottage. It's a soup. But on the other hand, don't allow it to get too liquidy. You don't want some dish-water with floating cabbage in it, do you? You'll get a feel for what it is, anyway. Do heat and reheat several times before serving. It's great with parmesan sprinkled liberally on top too. Enjoy!

Take a Punt on the Boathouse

The Cherwell Boathouse is a restaurant with a difference, situated on the banks of the River Cherwell close to the centre of Oxford, offering diners the opportunity to experience a true Oxford tradition: punting!

As a well-established family-run business, The Cherwell Boathouse aims to provide good quality and good value food alongside a quintessentially Oxford experience.

Johnny Verdin took on this responsibility from his father Anthony, who purchased the premises in 1968 after falling for it while studying at the university (and camping out in the fields opposite during sale negotiations!) thanks to the picturesque riverside location. This also lends the restaurant its unique attraction: the punts.

Managed by Roger Forster for more than 30 years, the boathouse has a fleet of over 70 traditional hand-built Oxford punts, to which more are added every year from the on-site workshop.

Whether you're keen to get onto the water or content to watch the antics from indoors, or the al fresco dining space, punting on the river is "a timeless pleasure for anyone, from graceful experts to novices trying to navigate the river," says Johnny.

The restaurant is popular with locals, families, business people, tourists and couples; it's been hailed as one of the most romantic places to dine in Oxford, and even hosts a few proposals each year. With large outdoor spaces as well as the dining room and catering for weddings and special events, The Cherwell Boathouse is ideal for celebrating an occasion.

Between head chef Paul Bell and restaurant manager Brice Guibert, guests can be assured that the food and drink will be as memorable as the punting. There's a set menu, changing several times a year based on fresh seasonal produce, alongside the à la carte options and flexibility when it comes to dietary requirements.

Paul takes inspiration from the classics, reinventing them with personal touches based on his previous experience working in London, Melbourne and France. Brice looks after the restaurant's award-winning wine list, which features some great value fine wines, many sourced in the 90s when Anthony was also running a wine import business.

"My father loved his food and wine, as well as having the foresight to buy lots of good vintages where he found them," says Johnny. The Cherwell Boathouse holds regular tasting evenings, where six courses are matched with various wines, sometimes focusing on a particular region or grape, which people in the know are always very keen to visit for.

"We like to think of ourselves as a fine dining establishment, but in a relaxed atmosphere," explains Johnny, "and hope to continue my father's legacy here for as long as possible."

Breaded Halloumi, Avocado, Sweetcorn Fritter, Lime

This colourful dish is great to make for an impressive brunch, or a light and summery lunch with plenty of flavour.

Preparation time: approx. 25 minutes, plus chilling | Cooking time: approx. 15 minutes | Serves: 4

For the breaded halloumi
2 blocks of halloumi, halved lengthways
100g plain flour & 4 eggs, beaten
300g panko breadcrumbs

For the lime gel
250g lime juice
125g caster sugar & 7g agar agar

For the avocado emulsion
200g avocados & 2 limes, juiced
2g salt & 75g cold-pressed rapeseed oil

For the sweetcorn fritter
50g unsalted butter
450g raw sweetcorn
100g self-raising flour

10g fine sea salt & 2 eggs
½ bunch of fresh coriander, chopped

For the smoked sweetcorn salsa
2 cobs of sweetcorn, in husks
1 red pepper & 1 banana shallot
1 red chilli & 1 tomato
1 lemon & ½ bunch coriander, chopped

For the breaded halloumi

Turn the pieces of halloumi in the flour until lightly covered, then dip in the beaten egg to coat, letting the excess drip off. Next, place in the breadcrumbs and gently shake off the excess. Finally, repeat the process just with the egg and breadcrumbs to make sure each piece is fully coated. Cook the breaded halloumi in a deep fryer, or a large pan half full of vegetable oil, at 180°c until golden brown which should take about 3 minutes. Place on a plate lined with kitchen roll to absorb excess oil.

For the lime gel

Place all the ingredients in a saucepan and bring to the boil. Chill and whisk to create a gel-like consistency. Transfer the gel into a squeezy bottle and keep in the fridge until serving.

For the avocado emulsion

Place the avocado flesh in a blender with the lime juice and salt. While the mixture is blending, slowly add the rapeseed oil to create an emulsion. Transfer into a squeezy bottle and refrigerate.

For the sweetcorn fritter

Melt the butter then lightly whisk all the ingredients together. Place spoonfuls of the mixture into a small ovenproof pan on a medium heat. Once the fritters are two thirds cooked through (you will see them firm up around edges) flip them over and place the pan in a preheated oven at 180°c for 3 minutes. You may need to do this in batches so the pan isn't too crowded.

For the smoked sweetcorn salsa

Cook the sweetcorn and red pepper for 5 to 7 minutes on a hot barbecue with the lid on to keep the smoke in. Meanwhile, finely chop the shallot and chilli then sweat them in a frying pan. Chop up the barbecued pepper and remove the sweetcorn from its husk, slicing down the cob to take the kernels off. Dice the tomato then mix all the ingredients together with a squeeze of lemon juice and season with salt.

To serve

Squeeze some avocado emulsion around the plate. Place a sweetcorn fritter in the centre, top it with a piece of breaded halloumi then two tablespoons of the salsa, and finish with a drizzle of lime gel.

Life Is What You Bake It

Christine Wallace has loved baking and cooking for as long as she can remember, but since appearing on The Great British Bake Off she has also enjoyed sharing her skills and knowledge in various ways across her home county of Oxfordshire and beyond.

In 2013, a baker with a passion for beautifully decorated cakes, who hadn't thought she'd even get an audition, became a Quarter Finalist on The Great British Bake Off. Christine Wallace had planned to apply a year earlier, but a serious illness hospitalised her and badly affected her confidence, making it difficult to leave the house and almost impossible to imagine ending up on a TV show watched by millions.

However, with her niece's encouragement, Christine reluctantly filled out an application form, which she forgot about completely until a call came out of the blue some months later. Auditions followed, Christine passed every stage, and having "summoned up every bit of courage to see the journey through, Bake Off gave me my life back."

She has had "a fabulous time ever since" doing many different things relating to food, cookery and baking, from demonstrations at festivals and events such as WI talks to regular airtime on Radio Oxford and Berkshire.

One of her most nerve-wracking yet rewarding experiences was cooking for members of the Royal Family! Christine also teaches cookery and baking, offering flexible lessons for small groups of up to five people in her cosy kitchen at home. She describes them as "very personalised and a lot of fun" with an emphasis on whatever people are keen to make. You can book online or buy a gift certificate which is always a popular option.

Christine organises Didcot Food Festival, which brings together around 60 food and drink contributors plus celebrity chefs in the demonstration theatre. The festival is held each October in the Civic Hall, and all the money raised goes towards Didcot's long-running annual Street Fair, which includes a themed parade.

Christine got involved with the events committee after her appearance on The Great British Bake Off and developed the festival to help fund the street fair.

"I've met a lot of people that I never would have otherwise, been asked to do so many different things, and had a ball really," says Christine of her journey after Bake Off.

"I was invited to a shop opening recently and that reminded me of how much I enjoy public events, because I just love people. It's an enormous pleasure to pass on the skills I've learnt and all the knowledge I've gained, which were probably doubled during Bake Off and which haven't stopped growing since!"

Summer Fruit Roll with Lemon Mascarpone Cream

I have made my own lemon curd for this recipe, but you can use a good quality ready-made one if you wish. For the fresh fruit, any combination of strawberries, blackcurrants, redcurrants, raspberries, blackberries and blueberries would work well.

Preparation time: 20 minutes, plus overnight | Cooking time: 15 minutes | Serves: 6

600g fresh berries
100g caster sugar
6 slices of slightly stale white bread

For the lemon mascarpone cream

2 medium unwaxed lemons, zested and juiced
85g caster sugar
45g unsalted butter
½ level tsp cornflour

1 large egg
1 egg yolk
125ml double cream
100g full-fat mascarpone

To garnish

A sprig of mint
A sprinkling of sieved icing sugar

Reserve a few berries for decoration and place the remainder in a pan with the caster sugar. Gently bring to a simmer and cook for about 5 minutes. Do not stir vigorously or crush the fruit. Strain the fruit thoroughly through a fine sieve over a bowl and leave until all the syrup has left the fruit. Meanwhile, lay out six squares of cling film on the work surface and cut each slice of bread into a square, removing the crusts as you do. Pour most of the fruit syrup into a dish or plate and thoroughly coat each slice of bread on both sides. Lay each slice on a square of cling film, leaving a spare inch or so at one end.

Spoon some fruit onto the bread about an inch up from the bottom of the slice, adding enough fruit to create a filling, but not so much that it squeezes out when rolled! Roll the bread tightly around the fruit like a swiss roll, using the film to help. Twist the extra cling film at either side to enclose the roll, then secure the ends with bag ties. Refrigerate the summer fruit rolls overnight.

For the lemon mascarpone cream

First, make the lemon curd. Add the lemon zest and juice, sugar, butter and cornflour to a bowl over a pan of simmering water, then stir until dissolved. Take off the heat.

Beat the whole egg with the yolk then pour into the lemon mixture while whisking vigorously. Place back on the heat, stirring constantly until the curd has just thickened. Do not over heat otherwise the mixture will curdle. Set the lemon curd aside to cool by placing the bowl in cold water.

Meanwhile, whip the cream until soft and thick but not stiff. Gently beat the mascarpone and cooled lemon curd together until smooth, then fold in the whipped cream (the mixture will thicken).

To serve, carefully unwrap the rolls, trim the edges and lay on serving plates. Brush some of the reserved syrup over each roll to give them a nice glaze. Arrange your reserved fresh berries, then either quenelle or pipe some of the mascarpone cream onto the plate. Spoon over a little more syrup then top with the mint sprig. Dredge the fruit with icing sugar and serve immediately.

The Perfect Catch

Cuttlefish brings the best sustainable seafood to Oxford, offering an informal yet delicious dining experience that celebrates the bounty of both English and Mediterranean coastlines.

Yola Drage and Alberto Brunelli, owners of the much-loved neighbourhood restaurant La Cucina, had a surprising opportunity presented to them in 2016 when the fish restaurant on St Clement's Street closed down, leaving an empty space right next door to La Cucina.

The couple decided to take it on, lending their strong brigade and experience in the trade to the new venture, which launched as a seafood bar and grill, which they called Cuttlefish. La Cucina customers began visiting Cuttlefish regularly, alongside Oxford's many tourists and even the Italian restaurant's staff: each business has a core team but supports the other by working flexibly, sharing resources where needed so both can flourish.

It certainly proved successful as word spread, and the seafood theme soon evolved to include brunch, lunch, snacks and coffee over the morning and afternoon. For evening visits, the mouth-watering menu combines the Mediterranean influences of head chef Michele Genna, who is from Sicily, with the freshest daily catch sourced from his supplier in Brixham.

Often the fish available is down to the supplier's recommendation, as the chefs will always be on the phone in the evening discussing the best produce to cook tomorrow.

Some of the most popular dishes include squid ink spaghetti with mixed seafood, rich and aromatic Mediterranean fish soup, freshly steamed mussels done three ways, generous bowls of paella and River Yealm oysters from Devon.

You can, however, opt for the ultimate traditional favourite with fish, chips and mushy peas, or prove yourself a true seafood lover with the luxurious platters alongside grilled lobsters or hot pot of clams and mussels.

The talent and care of the kitchen team is matched by Yola's front of house staff, who are "charming yet very friendly, because we aim for our service to be informal and relaxed so diners can enjoy themselves, as well as eating top quality seafood at the fairest prices we can set."

Some of these staff come back to Cuttlefish after doing work experience in the restaurant. Being involved with schools and running apprenticeships is important for Yola and Alberto, not only to find people who genuinely love the job, but to be part of the community that supports them in turn.

"Our aim is for Cuttlefish to enter the Hardens guide," says Yola., "We want to get our names out there of course, but also put St Clement's on the map because it's a wonderful part of Oxford and we love having our restaurants here."

Mediterranean Fish Soup

We like to serve this with homemade focaccia, sliced and toasted with garlic butter then sprinkled with fresh parsley. It's great for soaking up all the lovely juices. Scampi refers to langoustine or Dublin Bay prawn tails here, not the battered seafood you might have had before!

Preparation time: 10 minutes | Cooking time: 35-40 minutes | Serves: 4

50ml olive oil

2 sprigs of rosemary, finely chopped

Handful of fresh basil leaves

Handful of fresh parsley, chopped

1 red chilli, finely chopped

1 red onion, finely chopped

1 spring onion, finely chopped

2 cloves of garlic, crushed

100ml white wine

8 small squid, cleaned and sliced

200g plum tomatoes, chopped

600ml fish stock

8 large peeled prawns

24 fresh clams, closed and cleaned

24 fresh mussels, closed and cleaned

400g white fish fillets (monkfish is good due to its firm texture)

Sea salt and freshly ground black pepper

4 scampi, for garnish

Heat the olive oil in a large saucepan then add the herbs (setting a little parsley aside for garnish) along with the fresh chilli, onions and garlic. Sauté these ingredients for 5 minutes on a medium heat. Pour over the wine and simmer until evaporated. Add the squid and the tomatoes. Pour in the fish stock, bring to the boil and simmer for 15 minutes.

Add the prawns, clams, mussels and white fish to the pan and simmer gently for about 7 minutes. Discard any mussels or clams that did not open, then taste the soup. Season if necessary to taste.

On the side, cook the scampi in a ladle of the soup. These are cooked separately so they don't get damaged and look lovely as a garnish. They are very quick to cook, so 2 minutes should suffice. Meanwhile, toast the garlic bread, sprinkle it with fresh parsley and place on the edge of the bowls of fish soup. When they are cooked, place the scampi on top of the soup to garnish and serve.

Chef's tip

If you are able, it is a good idea to open up the clams separately in a pan on the stove. Simmer them with garlic, parsley and a little water and white wine. It should only take 2 minutes for the clams to open. The reason for this is to ensure that the clams you add to the soup are free of grit and sand. Once the clams are open, you can sieve the sand away and discard the cooking liquid, then add them to the soup with the mussels and other fish.

Home Sweet Home

Jolly Good Brownies is what the name suggests and more: irresistible squidgy chocolate indulgence, made to order and delivered to your door!

Oli Barton had been making brownies "forever" for friends, family and clients when a next-door neighbour suggested she turn the treats into a new business venture. Having been a caterer for many years, and a trained chef, Oli felt that going back to all the evenings and weekends of work with her three children now in the picture just wasn't appealing.

So, instead, she set up Jolly Good Brownies from home in 2018 and began a mail-order service that delivers her brownies right across the UK.

Using her original recipe as the starting point, Oli developed more flavours and varieties to offer something for everyone. You can now choose from salted caramel, chocolate orange, Toblerone, gluten-free and low-sugar brownies for children, as well as raw vegan fruit and nut bars, which you can find the recipe for over the page!

Jolly Good Brownies make great presents as they come gift wrapped, and can be sent anywhere in the country. The ordering process is all online, and there are gift boxes for various special occasions from birthdays to new babies (aimed at the sleep-deprived parents, of course!) although you can always treat yourself too.

The interest of local people, word of mouth, and then social media played a big part in growing sales for the fledgling company, alongside Oli's enterprising partnerships with other local independents. Her brownie boxes can include add-ons such as Neal's Yard products, hand creams from Oxford Soap Company and local clothing business White Coco's own scented candles, to make gifting more personalised.

Oli also has an important connection to Sobell House, as her mother-in-law "was cared for by the amazing team at Sobell House towards the end of her life, so the charity does have an important connection to our family."

All Oli's brownies are freshly made to order, using free range eggs and high quality ingredients to make them jolly good. The company name was suggested by a friend as 'Bloody Good Brownies' but when their son (then five years old) overheard wrongly while Oli and her husband were discussing it, he decided that Jolly Good Brownies was the perfect fit!

The company has certainly lived up to its name, having been shortlisted for the 2020 South Vale Business Awards as a New Startup, and Oli is hoping to expand in the near future, moving to a commercial premises and growing her current team of one so Jolly Good Brownies can reach more people...watch this space!

Raw Chocolate Orange Fruit and Nut Bars

When you taste these, you won't believe they are as healthy as they are. These nut bars are vegan, free from refined sugar, gluten-free and dairy-free and (I promise) just delicious. Even my children love them! What's more, they are so simple and quick to prepare...the hard part is waiting for them to set!

Preparation time: 10 minutes, plus 2 hours to set | Serves: 12

For the base
300g dried pitted dates
250g raisins
175g walnuts
2 tsp water
1 tsp orange extract (found in the baking section of most supermarkets)
6 tbsp cocoa powder

For the topping
2 tbsp coconut oil
25g cocoa powder
90g agave syrup (again, found in the baking section of most supermarkets)
¼ tsp orange extract

For the base

Line a tin or dish (roughly 25cm by 15cm) with baking parchment. Put all the ingredients for the base into a food processor and blend until everything is finely ground and the mixture has a dough-like consistency. Try not to over blend as this will make the mixture a little oily. Spread the base evenly into the dish and press down firmly.

For the topping

Melt the coconut oil gently in a saucepan. When melted, add the cocoa powder, agave syrup and orange extract then mix until smooth. Pour the topping over the base and spread out evenly.

Refrigerate the chocolate orange fruit and nut bars for 2 hours, then remove from the tin and cut into 12 pieces.

To serve

Delicious with a handful of fresh raspberries or strawberries.

Paul Chahidi's

Mediterranean Pork, Lemon and Parmesan Meatballs

One of my family's firm favourites, full of the flavours of the Mediterranean. The beauty of this dish is that it somehow manages to be both hearty and light. Quick and easy to make, if you don't have fresh herbs just use dried ones from the store cupboard. Bon appetit!

Preparation time: 20 minutes | Cooking time: 35 minutes | Serves: 4

500g pork mince
80g breadcrumbs
1 lemon, zested and juiced
A good handful of flat parsley leaves, roughly chopped
8 sprigs of fresh thyme, leaves stripped from the stems

80g parmesan
Salt and freshly ground black pepper
2 tbsp olive oil
500ml chicken stock
300g orzo pasta (approximately 75g per person)

Preheat your oven to 200°c. Place the pork mince and breadcrumbs in a bowl. Add the lemon zest and juice, reserving a pinch of zest for garnish. Add the chopped parsley, again reserving a generous pinch for garnish, and all the thyme leaves, then grate the parmesan into the mixture. Season with a couple of pinches of salt and a generous amount of freshly ground black pepper.

Thoroughly combine the ingredients using your hands and form 12 meatballs, approximately the size of golf balls.

Heat the olive oil in a pan and fry the meatballs in batches, until browned. Place the meatballs in a shallow ovenproof dish and add enough boiling chicken stock to reach halfway up the meatballs in the dish. Cook the meatballs in the preheated oven for 25 minutes.

Halfway through the cooking time, prepare the orzo pasta according to the packet instructions (usually this takes 8 to 10 minutes).

Drain the pasta and divide equally between four wide, shallow bowls. Add three cooked meatballs to each of the bowls and spoon a decent amount of the broth over the meatballs and orzo. Garnish with the reserved parsley leaves and pinch of lemon zest.

Serve with steamed greens (I usually have tenderstem or purple sprouting broccoli, or cavolo nero) and lemon wedges.

A Little Slice of Italy

La Cucina is as close to a true trattoria and pizzeria as you can possibly get in Oxford, offering a family-oriented experience with excellent, authentic Italian food at its heart.

Established by husband and wife team Alberto Brunelli and Yola Drage, La Cucina is a neighbourhood restaurant that brings people together over great food and an atmosphere of warmth that is usually found only in the home.

Its name, meaning 'kitchen', reflects the ways in which Yola and Alberto aim to create a home from home in their little restaurant: you walk into the waft of garlic, rosemary, rich sauces and freshly baked dough thanks to an open kitchen, complete with a pizza oven, that lets diners watch the chefs creating their meal. The feel is very informal and cosy, with boxes of wine tucked into corners and ingredients like pasta and biscotti lining the shelves, lending La Cucina elements of an Italian delicatessen and making food the focal point everywhere you look.

It was always the couple's goal to have their own business, since they both had an extensive education in the food and hospitality industry. Alberto is from Lombardy, near Milan, and has assembled a team of fellow Italians including his head chef Marcus Barreto, who has been with them almost since day one. Their knowledge and commitment to what Yola describes as "slow food" forms the building blocks of a menu celebrating authentic produce and fresh ingredients from a mixture of local and Italian suppliers, bringing the best of both worlds together.

La Cucina makes fresh pizza dough, pasta (including gluten-free varieties) and sauces alongside vegan dishes, daily meat and fish specials, and Alberto's risottos which are incredibly popular and regularly requested! The team have also done outside catering, and you can even dine in with their takeaway menu on Deliveroo, which recently added family-size portions of popular dishes.

The bar also stays true to Italian products, serving digestivo and grappa alongside real Italian coffee bought by a London-based supplier from a family-run business in Milan. La Cucina's ethos celebrates wonderful Italian flavours with ingredients that speak for themselves, so the owners also like to employ people who are genuinely passionate about food and can talk about the menu knowledgeably with guests to ensure everyone has the best experience possible.

Its accessibility - to families, residents, visiting academics, tourists - makes La Cucina a place of welcome that's all about eating and enjoying yourself. In 2019, it made the final for Best Family Restaurant and Best Team in the English Italian Awards, which meant a lot to Yola and Alberto because it recognised what they aspire to by producing authentic, delicious food for everyone.

Risotto Milanese con Osso Bucco

Risotto Milanese is a risotto king in its own right, but the richness of the osso bucco adds even greater grandeur.

Preparation time: 10 minutes | Cooking time: 35 minutes | Serves: 4

For the osso bucco
4 pieces of veal bone marrow, about 2cm thick
3 tbsp mixed fresh white breadcrumbs and grated fresh parmesan cheese
1 tbsp tomato paste

For the risotto Milanese
900ml beef stock
3 pinches of saffron, steeped in 2 tbsp boiling water
75g unsalted butter
1 small onion, finely chopped
1 piece of veal bone marrow, about 4cm thick
1 bay leaf
300g super fine carnaroli risotto rice
175ml white wine
25g parmesan cheese, freshly grated
Sea salt and freshly ground pepper
Freshly chopped parsley

For the osso bucco

Preheat the oven to 180°c. Place the pieces of bone marrow in a small roasting tin, sprinkle the parmesan and breadcrumbs over the marrow and place in the oven for about 25 minutes. The topping should become golden brown and the marrow will start to 'melt' in the oven. Remove some of the excess fat from the tin, then add the tomato paste to the remaining marrow juices and stir to create a sauce.

For the risotto Milanese

While the bone marrow is in the oven, put the stock in a pan with the steeped saffron (including the liquid) and simmer. Melt 50g of the butter in a large heavy pan, add the chopped onion and the veal bone marrow then cook gently until the onion is very soft, but make sure it doesn't brown. Add the bay leaf and the rice. Stir carefully on a medium heat until the rice is coated with the butter. Pour in the white wine then allow it to absorb into the rice. Add the hot stock — not all in one go, but ladle by ladle — and stir until mostly absorbed before adding the next lot. After about 15 to 20 minutes, when the rice is tender and moist and all the stock has been added, remove the pan from the heat and leave to rest for 30 seconds. Dice the remaining butter and gently stir into the risotto along with the parmesan. Season to taste with salt and pepper.

To serve

The consistency of the risotto should be *all'onda*; when plated the rice should move like a wave, all as one. Place the pieces of roasted bone marrow on top of the risotto, drizzle the marrow sauce from the pan lightly over the marrow bone, and finally sprinkle the dish with the freshly chopped parsley.

A Recipe for Success

Lotte Duncan wears many hats in the world of food and drink, but her most recent roles include director of Bradford on Avon Food & Drink Festival as well as a food writer, presenter and all-round authority on British cookery.

Lotte has been cooking since the age of six, and loves food every which way. Her experience in the food and drink industry ranges far and wide, from TV presenting to awards judging, and her established career as a food writer is testament to the knowledge she has built up.

Having trained early on in Cordon Bleu cookery, Lotte went on to run a catering business, a cookery school and a café alongside writing her own cookery book, Lotte's Country Kitchen, and appearing on many TV programmes. She started out with her own mini series, then became one of the Ready Steady Cook chefs, and has been a regular face on Food Network UK as well as many other shows including BBC's Countryfile.

Today, one of Lotte's main projects and responsibilities is running Bradford on Avon Food & Drink Festival with her partner, Jon Hackett. She takes care of the creative side of the food festivals: looking after sponsorship, the chefs, demonstration stage and more. Organising these popular events is a huge undertaking, and a lot of Lotte's time is spent choosing the stall holders, and sampling all new ones of course!

This means that high quality produce is guaranteed at the festival, and Lotte's contacts in the food industry ensure the demonstration stage is always brimming with culinary talent.

The festival was established to celebrate all that is delicious about the south west and showcases local and national produce for people to sample and enjoy. There is a Street Food Market, a wide range of artisan food, a stage for chef demonstrations and even a pop-up pub. Dogs are welcome too, making it a great event for families, and there are lots of shopping and sightseeing opportunities in the historic market town that hosts the festival each year.

Her work with Scrumptious Food Festivals, which encompasses two events in Bradford on Avon and Thame Food Festival in Oxfordshire, is informed by Lotte's role as the host of various stages for BBC Good Food Shows. This has taken her as far as Dubai and often finds her in conversation with some of the biggest names in food TV.

Since 2015, Lotte has also been a judge for the Great Taste Awards where she loves having the opportunity to discover brilliant brand new products, and in 2019 she joined Love British Food as one of their ambassadors.

Lemon and Basil Pasta

A delicious dish for a summer's day.... full of zingy citrus, aromatic basil, fragrant olive oil and salty cheese!

Preparation time: 5 minutes | Cooking time: 15 minutes | Serves: 4

3 large lemons
250g dried spaghetti
150ml extra-virgin olive oil
200g parmesan cheese, freshly grated
25g butter

A very large handful of fresh basil (be generous)
Salt and freshly ground black pepper
50g pistachios, chopped
Extra basil and grated parmesan, to serve

Peel the zest from one of the lemons in large strips. Zest the other two lemons with a fine grater, then juice all three lemons.

Boil a large pan of salted water with the strips of lemon zest in and cook the spaghetti according to the instructions but for 2 minutes less, so the pasta is al dente.

Mix the finely grated lemon zest and the lemon juice with the olive oil and parmesan. Once the pasta is cooked, melt the butter in a large saucepan and toss in the lemon sauce. Add the pasta and mix well with a little of the pasta cooking water.

Tear the basil up, stir in and season with salt and freshly ground black pepper. Serve the pasta sprinkled with the pistachios, basil and parmesan.

Holy Moley!

Those might just be your first words when you discover Toot Baldon's hidden gem; from wintry Sunday roasts to drinks in the sunlit garden, The Mole Inn is known throughout Oxfordshire as a top-notch spot for food, a friendly welcome and a beautiful setting.

The Mole Inn has been in Sarah Heather-Holt's family for a long time; she had always wanted to be involved in hospitality and jumped at the opportunity to join the family business in 2018. Sarah's only experience was helping out in her dad's other pub, The Mole and Chicken, so it was "a really fast learning curve," but one that led to great success. The new team under managers Johnny and Jess's guidance soon gained a second AA Rosette and in 2020 The Mole Inn was crowned Best Newcomer at the Ox In A Box Awards. It's earned a mention in many local food guides from Michelin to Hardens, but Sarah is equally proud of the support from locals in the village of Toot Baldon, where The Mole Inn is tucked away amidst beautiful countryside.

You almost have to be in the know to find this secluded spot, but luckily word has spread about the highly rated food which always features exciting twists, like the Thai spiced fishcakes which are a particular favourite with customers.

Pub classics like fish and chips, steaks (all dry aged and hung for a minimum of 28 days) and burgers can be found on the menu but are elevated with care and attention to detail as well as dishes that show chef Johnny's love of Asian food, such as Korean chicken wings and salt and pepper baby squid.

The Mole Inn uses a range of local suppliers, including Sandy Lane Farm for lamb and pork. It's also known for fresh fish, brought in daily from boats around the British coast and prepared immediately for the specials.

As a village pub, it has a tempting selection of local ales from Hook Norton, alongside seasonal offerings from breweries in Abingdon. With a varied wine list, cocktail menu and plenty of interesting gins, everyone can enjoy their favourite tipple. The beautiful garden is the perfect place to do this during summer, and in colder months a seat by the inglenook fireplace is hard to beat; the Grade Two listed building can't fail to make you feel super cosy.

Sarah is keen to preserve the family-run pub's special qualities, and loves to meet customers when she can be out in the bar or dining rooms. The rest of the success is down to her amazing team who work so hard to deliver the best food, service and welcome every day.

Going forward, Sarah wants to focus on environmentally friendly and sustainable practices, as well as involving the locals to make sure The Mole Inn remains a favourite place in the village to eat and drink.

Tuna Tartare with Avocado Purée & Black Garlic Mayo

This recipe was created by The Mole Inn's executive chef Johnny Parke. The delicately balanced yet full flavoured dish draws on Japanese influences alongside the French technique of making tartare, which simply means 'raw' and can be prepared with any top quality fresh meat or fish.

Preparation time: 15 minutes, plus 3 hours chilling | Serves: 4

For the black garlic mayo
4 tbsp Japanese mayonnaise
4 cloves of black garlic
1 tsp grated ginger
1 tsp rice wine vinegar

For the avocado purée
2 ripe avocados
1 lime, juiced
1 tsp rice wine vinegar

For the tuna tartare
400g sashimi-grade tuna
1 tbsp black & white sesame seeds, toasted
1 tbsp finely chopped coriander
1 tbsp finely chopped chervil
1 tbsp grated ginger
1 tbsp white miso
1 tbsp gochujang paste

1 tsp rice wine vinegar
1 tsp sesame oil
2 limes, juiced

To serve
Sourdough, thinly sliced and toasted
Radishes, thinly sliced
Picked herbs or baby salad leaves

When you're making all three elements, leave the salt and pepper until last and taste the mixtures before you add seasoning, because some of the ingredients in the tartare are already salty.

For the black garlic mayonnaise

Put all the ingredients into a small jug and blitz with a stick blender, taste and then season with salt and black pepper. Put the mayo into a squeezy bottle or piping bag and store in the fridge for a minimum of 3 hours. It will keep in the fridge for 1 month.

For the avocado purée

Remove the stone and skin from the avocados, put the flesh into a small jug, then add the lime juice and vinegar to the jug and blitz with a stick blender until completely smooth. Push the purée through a sieve if there are lumps. Taste and then season with salt and black pepper. Put the purée into a squeezy bottle or piping bag and store in the fridge for 1 hour. Best used fresh within 2 hours.

For the tuna tartare

Make sure the tuna is fridge-cold then dice into small cubes. Put these back into the fridge in a large glass bowl. Add all the remaining ingredients to another large bowl, then whisk until combined. Add the mixture to your diced tuna then season with salt and black pepper to taste.

Remember these are only guidelines; it's all about your personal taste and having fun.

To serve

I like to eat this with toasted sourdough, radishes and fresh herbs or salad leaves. To plate up, use my photo as an idea, or express yourself and give it your own personal touch. Enjoy.

Rising to the Occasion

Botley's independent artisan bakery was founded on the love of natural bread, as its name suggests, which is always freshly made by hand and available across Oxfordshire in shops, cafés and markets.

Natural Bread is owned and run by Claire Véry, who grew up in France and was surrounded by a love of food from an early age. She retained her fondness for the local markets with their irresistible aromas of freshly baked bread.

Her husband, William Black, shared her passion for natural homemade food and in particular for making real bread without any additives, so in 2006 they set up Appleton Farmers' Market and began perfecting their sourdough recipe. William gathered every book he could find on sourdough and travelled across Europe to seek inspiration from bakers in France, Italy and beyond. Soon they were completely selling out every market day and couldn't keep up with production from home, even when they brought a pizza oven in their garage back to life, until the business moved to a commercial bakery in Botley.

The first Natural Bread shop and café was opened in Eynsham, followed by the flagship venue in Woodstock, then another shop and café on Oxford's Little Clarendon Street. Add to that a successful wholesale business supplying breads, pastries and cakes to restaurants, cafés and stockists across Oxfordshire, and life became very busy for Claire and William.

Sadly, William passed away in December 2014, following a year-long battle with a brain tumour.

Determined to continue with the vision that had inspired him, Claire has kept William's love of good food, natural ingredients and family values at the heart of Natural Bread.

Recent years have seen a change in direction for the business with the closure of the bakery shops and the growth of the wholesale business, alongside an expanding network of stockists across the county and beyond. One thing that hasn't changed is the bread. There are only four ingredients in the signature sourdough: water, salt, flour from Wessex Mill in Wantage and the bakery's own starter culture.

"We use traditional slow fermentation techniques, letting the sourdough starter do its job over 48 hours. This is what gives our bread its really rustic charm and means it is brilliant for the digestion too," says Claire. The bakery also gets through hundreds of eggs from Mayfield Eggs in Witney for cakes and pastries, which then go on to wholesale customers and are also sold at the local farmers' markets in Oxford every weekend.

Most recently, Natural Bread has launched an order and collect service, giving customers the option to order from their range and collect from Natural Bread market stalls, serving the Oxford community and showing that the well established company has not forgotten its roots while rising to success.

NATURAL
BREAD

An independent family run artisan bakery

Financiers

Claire Véry, owner of Natural Bread, celebrates her French heritage with this classic financier recipe: a real favourite with our customers. We like to follow tradition, using individual moulds in the shape of a small rectangular loaf and decorating simply with flaked almonds. You can however use cupcake cases if you only have these to hand.

Preparation time: 15 minutes | Cooking time: 28 minutes | Serves: 7

250g caster sugar
140g butter or plant-based spread,
melted
4 eggs
½ tsp vanilla extract
40g gluten-free flour
250g ground almonds
Handful of flaked almonds

Preheat the oven to 180°c. In a mixing bowl, cream the sugar and melted butter or spread together. Beat in the eggs and vanilla extract, then fold in the flour and ground almonds.

Divide the mixture evenly between paper cupcake cases. Sprinkle with flaked almonds, then bake the financiers in the preheated oven for 28 minutes. They should be golden brown and springy to the touch. Leave to cool then serve in the paper cases.

Pushing the Boat Out

No.1 Ship Street is an independent, modern British brasserie in Oxford city centre. It brings together top quality produce, a great location and vibrant atmosphere for the enjoyment of every guest.

Ross Drummond and Owen Little have worked in hospitality for 25 years and know Oxfordshire well. When a site on Ship Street in Oxford city centre became available in 2017, it was just what they had been looking for. After a substantial refurbishment they went into business with Ross front of house and Owen in the kitchen. They opened in July 2017 and the restaurant quickly gained in popularity.

No.1 Ship Street was voted Best Restaurant at the 2020 Ox In A Box Awards, has had an AA rosette three years running and won Best Opening at the Oxford Times 2018 Restaurant Awards.

"We hit the ground running and were lucky to find this great city centre location, which didn't offer many other independent restaurants at the time," says Ross.

Their success is also due in no small part to the food, which focuses on really good quality seafood delivered from Devon and Cornwall. Shellfish, oysters and fish dishes sit alongside seasonal fare from game suppliers and fresh produce from Cotswold Park. "Our menu isn't about foams and fancy garnishes; it's just really tasty food and the quality of the ingredients we source means that there's not much you need to do to make them taste amazing."

Complementing the generous platefuls, a lively atmosphere pervades both floors of No.1 Ship Street so guests can enjoy not just the food and drink but also the ambience. Originally the upstairs space was a champagne and oyster bar, but as the restaurant became busy enough, the downstairs brasserie encompassed the whole venue.

There's a team of around twenty, all under the direction of Ross or head chef Owen Little so they can ensure high standards are met. "We wanted to create a space that people enjoy coming into, that looks and feels welcoming. It's not just about the food or the service, it's about the whole experience," explains Ross.

The restaurant also offers a creative cocktail list alongside fine and rare wines, grower champagnes and premium spirits. The wine list focuses on small family-run vineyards and independent suppliers, biodynamic and natural wine making. As with everything at No.1 Ship Street, quality is key.

Recently, Ross and Owen created a private dining room within the restaurant, which is available to book for events such as conferences and special occasions. They are always looking ahead to the next steps for the venture and look forward to maintaining No.1 Ship Street's great reputation in Oxford and beyond.

French Onion Soup

Developed by Owen Little, this classic dish has been a staple on our menu since we opened in 2017. It's relatively straightforward, relying on the quality of the ingredients (especially the stock) and patience. Rushing this recipe will undoubtedly sacrifice depth of flavour, but done properly it is worth waiting for.

Preparation time: 10 minutes | Cooking time: 3 hours | Serves: 3-4

150g unsmoked streaky bacon, cut into lardons
½ a split pig's trotter
4 large white onions, peeled and thinly sliced
10 cloves of garlic, peeled and thinly sliced

1 tbsp caster sugar
200ml dry white wine
2 litres good quality beef stock
3 bay leaves
½ a bunch of thyme, finely chopped
1 tbsp redcurrant jelly
1 tbsp cornflour (optional)

50ml Cognac
Salt and black pepper
1 white baguette (or other bread)
Olive oil
100g Gruyère cheese, grated

Put the bacon and split pig's trotter into a large, heavy-bottomed saucepan over a medium heat, stirring until nicely browned all over. Remove from the pan and set aside.

In the same pan, cook the sliced onion, nine of the garlic cloves and the sugar. Stir occasionally. The onions will release a lot of liquid but keep cooking until all the liquid has evaporated and they are a dark brown, not quite burnt. Do not be tempted to rush this stage; it will take some time but a longer, slower caramelisation will give greater depth of flavour to the finished dish.

Now add the wine and deglaze. Add the stock, bacon, trotter, bay and thyme. Turn down to a low heat and simmer for 1 and a half to 2 hours. As it simmers, fat will rise to the top, so skim away with a ladle. The liquid will reduce by a quarter; remove the trotter and bay and discard them.

Add the redcurrant jelly and stir until dissolved. At this stage the soup may have a ring of fat on the surface. Some of this will soak into the crouton later and add flavour, however if you prefer to remove this you may use the cornflour. Mix the cornflour in a small bowl with a touch of water. Simply stir this into the soup while simmering and it will stop the fat appearing on the surface, as well as thickening the soup slightly. Now add the Cognac and season to taste with salt and pepper.

For the croutons, cut one slice of baguette or bread per person, roughly 1cm thick, and slightly smaller in diameter than the bowls you will be serving the soup in. Place the slices on a baking tray, spread the remaining slices of garlic over them, drizzle with olive oil and sprinkle with salt. Place the tray in a hot oven (180°c) for about 12 to 15 minutes, turning the croutons over halfway through, until well browned on both sides. Finally, pour the soup into bowls (preferably a classic soup terrine) and lay the croutons on top. Sprinkle each one with the Gruyère, then place under a hot grill until the cheese is melted and bubbling. Serve immediately.

Stephen Fry's
Bless Pots!

It's very satisfying to make hummus. So easy, but so satisfying. You will need a food processor or blitzer of some kind.

Preparation time: 10 minutes | Serves: 2-4

400g tin of chickpeas, drained
½ tsp bicarbonate of soda
55ml tahini
½ lemon
1 tbsp extra-virgin olive oil
2 cloves of garlic
1 tsp ground cumin

Generous pinch of salt
A few twists of black pepper
2 tbsp ice cold water
Pinch of paprika or cayenne pepper

If, as is likely, you're using tinned chickpeas, it's a good idea to boil them with the bicarbonate of soda for 20 to 25 minutes. Absolutely not necessary but it helps with creaminess and general taste. Cover the chickpeas with boiling water in a saucepan and add the bicarbonate of soda. Bring to the boil, then reduce the heat to a simmer and leave for about 20 minutes.

Drain the chickpeas in a sieve or fine colander and rinse them under the cold tap until the water runs clear, then pop them in a food processor.

Measure out your other ingredients; use a little less tahini than called for above if it's quite thick, but don't sweat about it. You can always thin the hummus with ice cold water while mixing. Juice the lemon (I sometimes zest the lemon first and add that too: no need if you're in a hurry, I'm just mad about lemon zest). Remember the garlic is raw so use fewer than two cloves if you think that will be too much for some people.

Add the tahini and lemon juice (plus the zest if applicable) to the food processor along with the olive oil, garlic, cumin, salt and pepper. Blitz until smooth (it may take longer than you think). Stop every now and again to scrape down the sides of the bowl with a rubber or silicone spatula. When it's just about done and with the processor still blitzing, drizzle in the two tablespoons of ice cold water. You can add more if the mixture is still too thick.

This hummus looks and tastes so good dusted with red cayenne pepper or paprika, and with a puddle of almost green extra-virgin olive oil on top. Serve with warm pitta bread or whatever the heck you want.

Sticking to your Roots

Mike North had known Nut Tree Inn nearly all his life, since his dad was born a couple of doors down the road and his grandmother had always lived in Murcott, but he didn't expect living and working at the village pub to become his future too...

Imogen and Mike North were both working in hospitality, running a pub as chef and manager respectively when they decided that given the chance, they wanted to open their own place together. Once they had found a unique venue in the village of Murcott, the couple bought the Nut Tree Inn freehold in 2006, and by 2008 they had gained a Michelin star which remains one of the pub and restaurant's many accolades to this day.

The 15th century Grade Two listed building has been a labour of love for Mike and Imogen, who live on site with three children and continue to invest all their skills and experience in the venture. They have added a dining room, a bespoke kitchen, an outdoor bar on the terrace and plenty of shine to the inn's reputation. Their ethos is to operate very much as a village pub, creating a warm and friendly atmosphere in the cosy indoor spaces for drinkers and diners alike, and the large garden is set aside purely for guests popping in for a pint.

Equal emphasis goes on the food and drink, from premium wines by the glass to the Loch Duart salmon that's oak-smoked in-house. Whether it's destined for the tasting menu or an à la carte option, every element of each dish is made from scratch in the inn's kitchen. There is always a balanced choice of meat, fish and vegetarian starters and mains, with sweets such as sticky toffee pudding served with caramelised apple (a real customer favourite) and cheeseboards to follow. Tasting menus can be paired with a carefully curated wine flight, and the distinct characters of the hand-picked real ales on draught provide something for everyone.

"None of our menus or drinks choices are exhaustive, because the whole point is to retain integrity and quality across the board," explains Mike. "We pick produce that works in harmony for all our dishes, sourcing the best and preparing it simply but in a way that you probably wouldn't do at home, so our customers can enjoy dinner out as a real treat."

Despite the challenges that come with running a small and very personal pub alongside raising their children, Mike and Imogen are confident and positive about the future of Nut Tree Inn. "We've been here for 14 years and had bumps in the road, but we've got through them and we're very proud of what we do."

Pig's Head & Black Pudding Terrine with Piccalilli

This is a perfect dish for the adventurous weekend cook, because although it may seem complex there is far more time than skill needed to create it. A butcher should be able to prepare the pig's head for you: the cheeks, snout and jowls are the parts worth using here.

Preparation time: 1 hour 45 minutes plus 24 hours for the piccalilli | Cooking time: 10 hours | Serves: 6

For the pig's head
1 pig's head, meat from the cheeks/snout/jowls picked (ask your butcher)
3 pinches of ground mace
3 sprigs of thyme & 3 cloves of garlic
2 pinches of salt
1 pinch of cayenne pepper

For the terrine
25g wholegrain mustard
35ml sherry vinegar & 100g black pudding

For the piccalilli
1 large white onion & 3 large carrots
1 small cauliflower & 1 cucumber
50g table salt & 100g sugar
500ml white wine vinegar

75g English mustard
20g fresh ginger, peeled and sliced
3 tbsp turmeric & coriander seeds
1 tbsp fennel seeds
1 small chilli, deseeded and sliced
1 clove of garlic, crushed
1 pinch of allspice & 1 star anise
6g agar agar

For the pig's head

In a large tray, combine the meat with all the remaining ingredients. Leave to marinate for an hour, then seal the meat in a large bag, ensuring there is no air. Place the bag in a large pan of water preheated to 83°c and cook for 10 hours, then leave to cool slightly before flaking the meat and discarding any large fatty pieces.

For the terrine

In a large bowl, mix the flaked pig's head meat with the mustard and vinegar. Adjust the seasoning with salt and pepper to taste. Put half of the meat into a 14cm by 8cm by 8cm plastic food container and press down lightly to flatten the mixture. Crumble the black pudding over the top, then add the rest of the meat. Using another plastic container, press firmly down. Place this in the fridge with a heavy weight placed on top to press the terrine as it cools. Once cool, remove the terrine from the container and slice into six equal portions about 1cm wide.

For the piccalilli

Peel and chop the onion and carrot into 1cm dice. Break the cauliflower into florets of roughly the same size, then deseed and dice the cucumber. In a large bowl, mix all the vegetables with the salt and leave for 12 hours to cure. Put all the remaining ingredients except the agar into a large saucepan with 250ml of water over a medium heat. Bring to the boil, then remove from the heat and leave to cool.

Rinse the cured vegetables under cold water in a large colander for 10 minutes to wash off any excess salt, then drain thoroughly. Strain the cooled pickling liquor through a fine sieve over the cured vegetables. Stir to mix thoroughly and leave to pickle for a minimum of 12 hours.

Strain the piccalilli liquor into a large saucepan, add the agar and bring to a fast boil over a high heat. Leave to cool for the agar to set firm. Blend the set piccalilli jelly into a smooth glossy purée. Reserve 100g of the purée and stir the remainder through your piccalilli.

To serve

In a large frying pan on a medium heat, fry the terrine slices for 1 minute on each side until golden brown. Transfer them to plates with a palette knife then arrange the piccalilli and purée around them. We serve this with English breakfast radishes, micro celery leaves and deep-fried quail's eggs.

Life of Thai

Oli's Thai is a neighbourhood restaurant with a well-deserved reputation for fantastic food, thanks to its owners and creators who have given everything, from the decor to the menu, a unique appeal.

After four years of searching, Ru and Ladd Thurston found the perfect site in the perfect location to open their own restaurant. They had both worked in restaurants and knew what they wanted, as well as what to avoid, so drew up detailed plans while holding down full time jobs and raising two young children. Ladd is Thai and the couple met in a Thai restaurant, so that was always going to be their focus, but they gained valuable experience by holding dinner parties and catering for people they knew. Eventually they had an opportunity to run the lunch service at Worton Organic Garden, and during that time, found their venue.

The renovation period was intensive, but friends and family chipped in to help make their vision a reality, and Oli's Thai (named after their son) opened in August 2014. Because they didn't want to be overwhelmed at first, Ru and Ladd hadn't advertised apart from telling the neighbourhood, but over the next few months, the small restaurant moved from a quiet, laid back start to a surge in popularity as word spread, and suddenly it was booking up three months in advance.

"I don't think we could have made it work like that straightaway, but because it evolved naturally things have worked out really well," says co-owner Ru.

Ladd heads up the kitchen, and is currently training Chloe Fella to be her head chef, who previously worked at Le Manoir aux Quat'Saisons and will take the reins so Ru and Ladd can move to executive roles. The food is rooted in recipes that Ladd grew up eating, made with European cooking techniques and tweaked according to how the couple like them. "There's no such thing as 'authentic Thai food' in our opinion, because not only regional but personal differences are everywhere and so you almost can't have the same dish twice," explains Ladd.

Reflecting this ethos, and aiming to incorporate seasonality, the menu at Oli's Thai changes every few weeks, with the exception of three dishes that have become the restaurant's signature: confit duck panang, aubergine curry and chickpea salad. These are enjoyed by incredibly loyal regulars; Ru and Ladd have become friends with lots of their customers because they visit so often.

"It's the restaurant we wanted it to be, really supported by the local community and small enough to stay manageable, but thankfully very popular."

Aubergine Curry

This has become the most popular dish in the restaurant. We wanted to do a twist on a red curry, using roasted European aubergines. We first cooked this for Ru's cousin and it remains her favourite dish to this day. Don't be scared to burn the edges, that's where the flavour is!

Preparation time: 15 minutes | Cooking time: 30 minutes | Serves: 4

For the paste

1 tbsp coriander seeds
Small pinch of cumin seeds
1 tbsp dried Dutch chillies, some
seeds removed
75g lemongrass, cut thinly across
25g galangal, cut thinly across
1 tbsp table salt

1 tsp ground white pepper
35g garlic, peeled
25g shallots, roughly chopped
40g big red chillies

For the curry

2 aubergines
8 tbsp vegetable oil
190ml coconut milk

30ml water or stock
80g fine green beans, halved
2 spring onions, cut into 3cm chucks
Handful of Thai basil
3 lime leaves, torn up
20g caster sugar
80ml coconut cream
50ml soy sauce

For the paste

Firstly, toast the coriander and cumin seeds in a frying pan over a low heat until golden. Once cool, put them in a spice grinder with the dried Dutch chillies and blitz to a fine consistency. With a pestle and mortar, pound a small quantity of the lemongrass and galangal together until smooth, adding more until you have used them all. Add the salt and pepper, then the other ingredients one at a time, pounding the mixture to a fine consistency before adding the next. Finally, add the blitzed dry spices and mix well. If you are using a blender to make the paste, add all the fresh ingredients and blitz until fine. Then add the coriander and cumin seeds, chillies, salt and pepper.

For the curry

Preheat the oven to 180°c. Prepare the aubergines, cutting each one lengthways into 10 or 12 wedges. For each wedge, cut along the flesh making a deep incision nearly reaching the skin and repeat, leaving 1 to 2cm gaps between each cut. Put them onto a baking tray and drizzle with five tablespoons of the vegetable oil. Roast for 25 to 30 minutes until soft but still holding their shape. Don't be alarmed if the edges burn slightly, this will give the finished curry extra flavour.

Put the remaining vegetable oil into a large pan on a low heat and add the curry paste. Cook the paste for a couple of minutes until you see the oil separate. Increase the heat and add the coconut milk, stock, green beans, spring onion, basil, lime leaves and sugar then cook for about 2 to 3 minutes while stirring continuously. Turn the heat down low, add the coconut cream and soy sauce, then simmer gently until the beans are cooked, which should take about 3 to 5 minutes.

Place the roasted aubergine wedges in a bowl and pour over the sauce. Garnish with basil leaves.

A Moveable Feast

Oxford Fine Dining has built up many strong working relationships over the years, not least with Sobell House for which it fundraises regularly alongside catering for some of the city's most prestigious venues and events.

Making and maintaining good relationships is at the heart of the Oxford Fine Dining ethos, and it's this commitment to clients and local suppliers that makes the catering company a preferred choice. They have an extensive portfolio of weddings, corporate events and private dining experiences, catering throughout Oxfordshire and the Cotswolds. Their chefs use innovation and creativity to ensure deliciously different menus at each special occasion and are extremely proud of the trusted reputation they have gained over the past decade.

Sue Randall co-owns Oxford Fine Dining with her business partner Della Hutton; they started the company in 2007 with firm roots in hospitality and a desire for excellence. Today, Sue describes her team as close-knit and runs Oxford Fine Dining very much like a family business. Customers might be attending a conference where the team have laid on a banquet for 1000 people, or enjoying canapés at a reception; the experienced caterers can provide "pretty much anything" including open fire cooking, which they introduced for the Shakespeare's Rose Theatre pop-up at Blenheim in summer 2019. Other highlights include catering for HRH The Prince of Wales, the Dalai Lama, The Rolling Stones and Countryfile presenters.

The chefs produce a menu for every season, making the best of local produce while allowing enough flexibility to ensure the food and drink is customised for each event.

In 2020, the team went out of their way to make this happen for a group of 200 local NHS volunteers, delivering afternoon teas to individual households with the help of their long standing suppliers. Each year, the caterers also participate in one of the city's most famous sporting events, the Oxford and Cambridge Boat Race, where they provide canapes for VIP spectators in London; this event is highly popular with the staff and clients alike!

Oxford Fine Dining also hosts an annual menu showcase to support Sobell House, as a member of the charity's Business Club. Each attendee donates £10 for the chance to win a catered dining experience at home, often raising over £1000 in total.

"We enjoy this event as it gives us a chance to catch up and thank our customers and suppliers, while showcasing what we do at our best," says Sue, "but we also want to give back to the community. When Sobell House got in touch, the more we spoke to friends and family the more we realised how many personal ties connected us to the hospice, so it just felt right."

OXFORD*fine*DINING

Chicken Breast, Pea Purée and Wild Garlic Hollandaise

This is a great dish that encapsulates spring, when aromatic wild garlic aromas are in full force and English asparagus is starting to appear.

Preparation time: 20 minutes | Cooking time: 30 minutes | Serves: 4

4 skin-on chicken supremes
Salt and pepper
300g butter
4 egg yolks
30ml white wine vinegar
100g wild garlic, finely chopped
400g peas

50ml rapeseed oil
12 asparagus spears

Season the chicken with salt and pepper then place skin side down into a lightly oiled hot frying pan. Seal for 30 seconds before transferring the pan to a preheated fan oven at 180°c for 30 minutes.

While the chicken is cooking, prepare the accompaniments. Melt the butter in a saucepan and skim off any white solids from the surface to clarify it. Keep the butter warm.

Bring a pan of salted water to a simmer (this will be used to cook the asparagus later). Sit a bowl over the pan and put the egg yolks into the bowl. Add the vinegar, whisking continuously. As the yolks start to cook, slowly whisk in the melted clarified butter, bit by bit, until it's all incorporated and you have a creamy hollandaise. Stir in the chopped wild garlic.

In a clean saucepan, combine the peas with the rapeseed oil and just cover with water. Cook for 5 minutes, then blitz to a purée.

Drop the asparagus spears into the salted boiling water (in the pan you used to make the hollandaise over) to cook for 1 minute, then serve up.

To serve

Put the pea purée around the edge of the plate, place the chicken in the middle with the asparagus next to it, then add the wild garlic hollandaise around the chicken. If you like, garnish with wild garlic flowers.

Spiced, Sealed, Delivered

Want delicious savoury or sweet delicacies delivered to your home, event or office? Look no further than Pindy's Samosas for parcelled-up perfection.

Pindy Basan had been making samosas for more than twenty years when, in 2017, she decided to set up a business selling them, because she really wanted everyone to experience the true taste of an authentic Punjabi staple. Each samosa is made to perfection, using specific processes for making the filling and pastry, shaping and frying that Pindy has experimented with and refined to create the best possible combination of textures and flavours. She was taught to make samosas by her mum, Kulwant, who would double check every stage to make sure Pindy's efforts met her high standards!

Thanks to this education, her understanding of both British and Indian cultures and the all-important original recipe, Pindy's Samosas has received nothing but fantastic feedback.

Customers can choose between flavours in boxes of five to twenty four, and whether they are looking for savoury or sweet there's something for everyone: Pindy has even created chocolate samosas and a mince pie special for Christmas, which she notes was one of her personal favourites.

"You just have to know what people want, and I love the satisfaction of providing quality products to people who appreciate good food," she says. Her vegetable samosa is always a clear winner though, which draws on the tried and tested family recipe.

Pindy's husband Surj (who has the envious job of chief samosa taster) supports her in developing the business. He also created the website, for which he had bought the domain years earlier when he found one with her name... almost as if it was meant to be!

Both individuals and companies can place orders online for any occasion. Pindy has catered for the University of Oxford and was also sponsored to provide nearly 100 samosas for Sobell House by Headington Market. She expertly juggles the deliveries, marketing and cooking but never takes shortcuts that affect quality, because her careful planning and attention to detail is crucial to getting the samosas right every time.

Samosas aren't the only trick up Pindy's sleeve though; she also makes pakoras (which are gluten-free) and other accompaniments including paneer spring rolls, chutney, chapatis and even homemade curries.

All of her food is vegetarian and most is vegan, including the original vegetable samosas. Having begun by selling mostly at markets in her local area, Pindy is now keen to expand the business beyond Oxford and Worthing. She is passionate about her food, and looking forward to what the future offers!

Chickpea and Red Pepper Curry

Chickpea curry is a popular Indian dish. I have added a twist with red peppers to give it a sweet taste. It's vegan, gluten-free and a quick and easy recipe.

Preparation time: 10 minutes | Cooking time: 30-35 minutes | Serves: 2

1 red bell pepper, chopped
3 tbsp rapeseed oil
2 medium onions, finely chopped
1 tsp cumin seeds
6 cloves of garlic, minced
1 tbsp minced ginger
½ tsp garam masala

½ tsp chaat masala
½ tsp ground coriander
1 tsp ground turmeric
½ tsp crushed red chilli
2 green chillies, minced (can be deseeded for less heat, use more or less to taste)

1 tsp salt
200g tinned chopped tomatoes
3 fresh tomatoes, finely diced
2 x 400g tins of chickpeas, drained and rinsed
Handful of coriander, for garnish

Temper the chopped red pepper in a hot pan for about 5 minutes until softened, then set aside.

To make the curry paste, heat a skillet over a medium heat and add the oil, onions and cumin. Temper for about 10 minutes, then add the garlic and ginger. Fry for about 4 minutes.

Add the spices: garam masala, chaat masala, ground coriander, turmeric, crushed red chilli and green chillies along with the salt. Stir to combine and cook for about 2 minutes.

Add the tinned tomatoes and fresh diced tomatoes. Cook for about 6 minutes until they are soft. Place the mixture into a blender, or use a handheld stick blender, then add a tablespoon of the drained chickpeas and blend until you have a smooth paste. Using some of the chickpeas here makes the sauce nice and thick.

Transfer the curry paste back to the pan and cook for 2 minutes over a medium heat. Add the remaining drained chickpeas and the tempered peppers with 150ml of water, then cook for a further 8 minutes. Turn the heat down to a simmer for a final 5 minutes.

Serve the curry with either homemade roti or basmati rice, garnished with fresh coriander.

Be Our Guest

You can chat to the cook in the kitchen and enjoy delicious food in the cosy dining room, but at The Secret Supper Society you won't be paying restaurant prices or doing the washing up!

The Secret Supper Society was established over twelve years ago, in a 'light bulb' moment for keen cook Jules. She came across the concept of hosting dinner for strangers at home while researching recipes, and instantly knew it was something she wanted to try. Three weeks later, her first evening went down a treat, and the venture took off very quickly as one of the UK's first supper clubs.

"I'm not a trained chef but I've always loved hosting dinner parties, so for me this was a natural progression that allowed a more artistic approach," says Jules.

The five or six course meals are hosted in the comfortable dining room of her farmhouse in North Oxfordshire, and always book up well in advance. Menus draw inspiration from a wide range of cuisines; Jules is motivated by the seasons and amazing local produce including cultured butter by artisan producer Grant Harrington, fresh loaves of sourdough bread from Forge House Bakery, and top quality meat supplied by Farmison & Co in Yorkshire. "I eat and sleep food, have a million cook books, and jot down new ideas constantly," she explains. "It's a full-time job to plan the courses around complementary flavour profiles, order ingredients, create a beautiful setting and prepare every element from scratch (down to the crackers for cheese and chocolates to finish) not least because I'm a complete perfectionist!"

Paying attention to the details within such a homely setting allows diners to experience a unique marriage of restaurant quality food, plus their own drinks with no corkage charge, and the relaxed atmosphere of a dinner party with friends. Jules and her husband Nick — who created The Secret Supper Society's branding and menu database (so that returning guests never have the same meal twice, unless they request it!) and is also the waiter — find that people love the element of surprise in not knowing what they'll be served, and often try things they would never have ordered but discover delicious new dishes in the process.

Jules has also hosted Woodland Pop-Ups and a Pop-Up Picnic, outdoor variations of her usual supper club, and previously donated dinners to Sobell House through a silent auction. She recently introduced a takeaway option which may continue past 2020, offering people the chance to enjoy a three course meal at home. Her flexibility as a one-woman enterprise has enabled The Secret Supper Society to thrive, bringing joy to adventurous foodies thanks to Jules' talent and genuine passion for welcoming guests to her 'home from home' restaurant.

Crab Linguine

This is a lovely quick supper dish, full of gorgeous flavours. You can either use all fresh crab meat, or to keep the cost down, mix 200g of fresh crab with a 200g tin of pasteurised crab meat. I like heat from my chillies, so I don't deseed them.

Preparation time: 5 minutes | Cooking time: 15 minutes | Serves: 4

2 tbsp table salt

2 tsp olive oil

50g butter

4 fat cloves of garlic, chopped

2 red chillies, chopped (and deseeded if preferred)

4 spring onions, sliced (including the green parts)

300ml white wine

6 ripe tomatoes, cut into wedges

400g dry linguine

400g crab meat

1 lemon, zested and juiced

20g fresh parsley, chopped

20g Grana Padano or parmesan, grated

Top tip: get everything ready before you start cooking. This is a quick dish and having all your prepped ingredients to hand will make it easier to get great results.

In a large pan, combine the table salt with four litres of water and bring to the boil. Test the saltiness; it should taste like the sea.

Gently heat a large sauté or frying pan (large enough to add your pasta to at the end) then add the olive oil and butter. Melt over a low heat, add the garlic and chilli then cook for a few minutes, being careful not to let it burn. Add the spring onions and cook for a couple more minutes.

Add the wine and reduce until it becomes almost like an emulsion. Add the tomatoes and cook until they start to break down. This should take about 8 minutes.

Meanwhile, add your linguine to the boiling salted water and cook according to the packet instructions. Make sure you reserve about 50ml of the salty water to add to your sauce while you are draining the cooked pasta.

Finally, add the crab, lemon zest and juice, parsley and pasta water to your garlic and chilli mixture, then tip the pasta into the pan as well and stir it through the sauce, making sure it's all coated. Sprinkle with the cheese just before serving. Pour yourself a glass of wine and enjoy!

Sue Perkins'
Jackfruit Wrap with Baba Ganoush

I should start by saying that I don't 'do' recipes. In fact, it's almost impossible for me to follow one without tweaking it, or going off at a strange tangent. In that spirit, NONE of these measurements need to be followed to the letter. Taste and adjust as you go, according to your palate. Enjoy!

Preparation time: approx. 20 minutes | Cooking time: approx. 20 minutes | Serves: 2 or more

For the flatbread
Cup of flour (I use spelt)
Large pinch of salt
Dash of olive oil

For the baba ganoush
As many aubergines as you have
Olive oil

1 tbsp tahini
1 clove of garlic, crushed
1 lemon, juiced

For the jackfruit filling
1 onion, finely sliced
1 clove of garlic, minced
A few sprigs of thyme and oregano

1-2 tins of young jackfruit in water
6 large tomatoes, roughly chopped
1 heaped tsp ground cumin
1 tsp sweet paprika, or more to taste
Pinch of chilli flakes
Pinch of sugar
Fresh parsley & coriander, chopped

Start by making the flatbread dough, which is so easy it's almost embarrassing. Get the flour and salt in a bowl, then add just enough water so that the mixture comes together into a ball. Add a splash of olive oil and transfer the dough to your countertop. Knead the dough until smooth and soft then set aside.

Then, on to the baba ganoush. Turn on the large gas ring to full. Put the aubergines directly onto the flame and nuke them until the skins are black and blistered. Transfer them to an ovenproof dish and let them cook fully until soft, 20 minutes or so at 180°c should do it. If you don't have a gas hob, prick the aubergines a few times with a sharp knife, place under a hot grill, then return to oven cooking once they're charred.

Now it's time to get your jackfruit filling started. Cook your onion until soft and translucent in as much oil as you prefer. Add your minced garlic, thyme and oregano (or use dried herbs if you don't have them) then cook for a further minute or so. Drain your jackfruit and add it to the pan along with your tomatoes (skin them first if you want to be posh). Turn the heat down to a gentle simmer. Now, add the cumin, paprika, chilli flakes, sugar and a pinch of salt to taste. Keep it all simmering while your aubergines cook.

Once the aubergines are done, rest them in a bowl until cool enough to handle. Remove the skins and drain off any excess liquid. Pop the flesh in a clean bowl, add a good glug of oil, some salt, the tahini, the crushed garlic and lemon juice to taste. I add some yoghurt for creaminess, but you don't have to. Adjust the seasoning to taste, then mash the mixture with a fork until the aubergines are broken down and the ingredients are well mixed. Pop into the fridge.

Back to the jackfruit. Load it with the chopped parsley and coriander. Taste and alter the seasoning to fit with what tastes delicious to you.

Finally, the flatbread. Get a pan on NUCLEAR heat. Portion up the flatbread dough, roll each portion out into a thin circle, and then chuck it into the pan once it's really hot. You should see bubbles forming on the top, which means it's ready to turn. Once it's charred and toasty on each side, it's ready to go.

To serve

Grab a flatbread. Load it with your jackfruit filling, a huge spoonful of baba ganoush and some freshly chopped lettuce. Fold in half. Scoff. Repeat.

Headshot: Steve Ullathorne

Buon Appetito!

SMEG is delighted to support Sobell House in the production of this book. With a longstanding heritage and expertise in producing beautiful cooking appliances, coupled with its local base in Abingdon, the company stands behind a cause which provides such a fantastic service to so many in the community.

Unlike many large international brands, SMEG remains staunchly family-owned and run, drawing upon its Italian roots for inspiration along the way. For SMEG, the kitchen is the real heart of the home, where good food is enjoyed and families come together. Based just ten miles from Sobell House, the brand's headquarters comprise a 'living kitchen' cookery school where its team of home economists develop and test recipes using SMEG appliances and cookware. This facility forms part of the company's wider showroom which you can visit by appointment.

Founded in 1948, the company began life specialising in metal smelting and enamelling until its founders spotted an opportunity to help automate people's kitchens in the post-war era when most were manual. Combining 'technology with style', as the tagline says, is the company's forte. Often referred to as the iconic Italian appliance manufacturer, SMEG embraces the culture of its home country to make good food and a beautiful kitchen the focal point of company philosophy.

This truly inspires design and production, from 50s style fridges, kettles, toasters, stand mixers and coffee machines to a vast range of ovens and range cookers. As you'd expect from an Italian brand, you can even authentically cook a pizza on a baking stone! The wide range of ultra-modern and retro products is designed to ensure customers can express their personality in the kitchen, whether that's with bright colours or a co-ordinated contemporary look.

In 2020, SMEG debuted its first ever range of 'smart appliances': ovens controllable via smartphone for ultimate convenience, which also include an in-built temperature probe and a self-cleaning mode. It's even possible to replicate the equipment of a professional kitchen at home with the trio of sous vide vacuum drawer, blast chiller and steam oven machines for the really ambitious home cook.

These indicate how passionate the company is about good food and innovation within the sphere of cookery, with an eye for detail that sets the products apart for many customers and gives the brand its unique character. SMEG even owns a parmesan cheese farm in Italy and uses this for tastings and demonstrations!

"We're passionate about supporting local causes where we can and investing back in the community we serve," says managing director Mike Giddings. "We are delighted to support such an amazing and worthwhile charity and have committed to sharing this book with our top customers and suppliers at Christmas."

Pizza

Create your own authentic pizza from scratch, with a golden, crispy base and melted cheesy top. This recipe is a fantastic dinnertime treat, suitable for the whole family to get involved and create their favourite pizza at home.

Preparation time: 5 minutes, plus 2 hours proving | Cooking time: 5 minutes | Serves: 4

175g strong bread flour
175g 00 flour
3 tbsp extra-virgin olive oil
15g fast acting yeast
Pinch of salt
200ml warm water
Passata
Your favourite toppings
Fresh rocket, to serve

Insert the dough hook attachment on a stand mixer. Add all the ingredients to the stand mixer bowl, except the water.

Begin mixing on speed two and add water gradually, until you achieve a soft and pliable dough. Knead in the stand mixer for 5 minutes.

Transfer the dough to a large oiled bowl and cover with cling film. Leave to rise in a warm place for approximately 1 hour, or until doubled in size.

After the first proving, divide the dough into four pieces. Put them on a tray – each positioned with plenty of room around them – and leave them until they double in size. This may take up to 1 hour.

Once the dough is ready, roll each ball out into a small circle. Using the weight of the dough, and the backs of your hands, stretch it out to create a large round disc.

Top the pizza base with passata, being careful to leave at least 1cm of uncovered dough on the edges of the circle to form a crust. Add your desired toppings, then put the pizza in a preheated oven at 250°c and cook directly on a preheated pizza stone for a few minutes.

To serve, slice with a pizza wheel and sprinkle over freshly torn rocket.

Pumpkin Risotto

Create this classic Italian dish with a colourful twist. Enjoy a combination of rich flavours with pumpkin and parmesan cheese in this beautiful creamy risotto. The perfect comfort food on a cold day, or as a delicious main to serve at a dinner party.

Preparation time: 10 minutes, | Cooking time: 1 hour | Serves: 4

1 large pumpkin, peeled and cut into 1cm cubes
Pinch of salt
2 tbsp extra-virgin olive oil
2 large shallots, thinly sliced
260g risotto rice
120ml dry white wine

600ml chicken stock, heated to a simmer
2 tbsp double cream
1 tbsp unsalted butter
1 tsp balsamic vinegar
Freshly ground black pepper
60g parmesan cheese

2 tbsp flat-leaf parsley, finely chopped

Place the pumpkin in a saucepan and cover with cold water, add a pinch of salt and simmer until tender. Once cooked, drain the pumpkin and add it to a blender with three tablespoons of water. Blend until smooth.

Heat the oil in a large saucepan over a medium-low heat. Add the shallot and cook until softened for around 5 minutes. Add the rice to the pan. Stir constantly until the rice is translucent, for about 5 minutes.

Add the wine and cook until it is mostly absorbed, then add 200ml of the stock and cook, stirring, until the liquid is mostly absorbed. Add another 100ml of stock and cook, stirring, until mostly absorbed. By this point the rice should be tender yet still slightly firm to bite.

Repeat until the stock is gradually absorbed. Add the blended pumpkin and stir to combine.

Stir in the cream, butter and balsamic vinegar then season with salt and pepper to taste.

To serve, divide the risotto between bowls, shave plenty of parmesan over the top and sprinkle with the parsley.

White Chocolate & Ricotta Mousse with Blueberry Sauce

A delicious summer mousse with delicate flavours of fresh blueberries and creamy white chocolate. The base of this recipe can be made in advance and stored in the fridge for up to 4 days, perfect for an easy dinner party dessert.

Preparation time: 5 minutes, | Cooking time: 5 minutes, plus 1 hour chilling | Serves: 4

100ml milk
150g white chocolate, broken into
chunks
300g ricotta cheese
100g pistachios, finely chopped
3 tbsp sugar
200g blueberries
Squeeze of lemon juice

Over a medium heat, bring the milk to a boil and pour it over the white chocolate. Stir until the chocolate has completely melted.

Add the ricotta cheese and mix well. Pour half of the creamy mixture into four cups, cover with the pistachios, reserving a few for garnish, and then fill each cup with the rest of the mixture.

Chill them in the fridge until ready for serving, or for at least 1 hour. Meanwhile, add the sugar, blueberries and lemon juice to a pan, simmer gently for a few minutes and then allow to cool.

To serve, garnish each cup with the blueberry sauce and the rest of the chopped pistachios.

Passionate about Provenance

The White Hart in Fyfield is a charming country dining pub that puts great food and hospitality at its heart. Often described as a foodie's paradise, it is a hub for both locals and visitors to gather, feast, relax and make memories.

Since arriving at the White Hart in 2005, Mark and Kay Chandler have restored this beautiful hostelry to its 15th century former glory. From the vaulted ceiling to the minstrel's gallery, this unique space is steeped in history.

As a family-run business, everything here is done with care, thought and passion and the impressive list of awards is testament to this.

"Mark and I fell in love with the White Hart when we first saw it and we are still passionate about what we do 15 years on," explains Kay.

"We are proud to be independent and support our community. We love the fact we grow our own produce and prepare everything fresh. We love that we make people happy. Quite simply, we have created the sort of experience that we like when we go out to eat."

The pub's modern British dishes are developed according to what's growing in the pub's kitchen garden and the surrounding countryside, as well as what's available on foraging expeditions. Mark heads up the culinary team; he began cooking when they took the pub on and were looking for chefs but no one they found was as good, so he decided to continue in that role. A year later The White Hart was awarded two AA rosettes for culinary excellence and he has never looked back!

By working with local farmers and suppliers alongside homegrown produce, new dishes can be created daily using the freshest seasonal ingredients. "This involves a lot of prep and is time consuming," says Mark, "but it's exciting for us and for the customers; they want to come back and see what is new, and our chefs are motivated by the creative opportunities."

Having said that, there's one dish that simply cannot be taken off the menu: the slow-roasted belly pork served with a foot long stick of crackling has become The White Hart's signature, and literally turns heads when brought through the dining room!

Of course, being a village pub, you can simply wander in for a pint as the locals do or enjoy a bite in the new outdoor dining space complete with wood-fired pizza oven.

Kay and her team are committed to making sure every visit, from a sit-down meal to a quick drink, is a wonderful experience for all their customers. From the warm welcome to the attention to detail, they do their utmost to ensure that each moment of your experience really hits the mark.

Elderflower Crème Brûlée with Gooseberry Compote

This is amazing when made in elderflower season using homemade elderflower cordial, but can be made all year round from good quality store bought cordial too. If you're feeling adventurous, try making the doughnuts to serve with the brûlée and compote.

Preparation time: 15 minutes, plus 2 hours proving | Cooking time: 30-40 minutes | Serves: 6

For the crème brûlée
400ml double cream
35g caster sugar, plus a little extra to brûlée
120ml elderflower cordial
6 egg yolks

For the gooseberry compote
400g gooseberries
6 tbsp caster sugar
2 tbsp elderflower cordial

For the doughnuts (optional)
210ml tepid milk
50g unsalted butter, softened
2 eggs, beaten
100g caster sugar
10g fresh yeast (or 5g dried)
300g plain flour
½ tsp salt
Vegetable oil, for frying

For the crème brûlée

Preheat the oven to 150°c. Place the cream, sugar and cordial in a pan. Heat gently until the sugar dissolves. Briefly beat the egg yolks in a bowl, then pour in the cream mixture while still beating. Pass through a sieve into a jug. Pour the mixture into ramekins (approx. 70ml in each) and place in a deep roasting tin. Fill the roasting tin with boiling water halfway up the ramekins. Place on the bottom shelf of the oven and cook for 30 to 40 minutes until just set. Remove from the oven and let the ramekins stand in the water for 10 minutes, then take them out and leave to cool.

For the gooseberry compote

Place the gooseberries, sugar and elderflower cordial in a pan and heat gently until the sugar dissolves. Bring to a simmer, cover and cook for 3 minutes, just until the gooseberries start to soften. Remove from the heat and allow to cool.

For the doughnuts (optional)

Combine the milk, butter, eggs and 40g of the sugar. Place the yeast in a small bowl, then add a little of the milk mixture to form a smooth paste (if using dried yeast add directly to the flour). Add this paste to the remaining milk mixture and whisk to combine. Place the flour and salt in a large bowl and make a well in the centre. Gradually pour in the milk mixture, whisking until smooth. Cover the bowl with cling film and place the dough in a warm spot to prove for approximately 1 hour or until doubled in size. Take the dough out and knock it back to remove the air, wrap in cling film and place in the fridge until cold. Roll the cold dough into 15g balls and place them on greaseproof paper squares to prove for a final 30 minutes. Place a large saucepan, one third filled with vegetable oil, over a medium heat until the oil reaches 170°c. Place the dough balls in the oil and cook for about 4 minutes, turning often, until golden brown and cooked through. Remove and drain on paper towels. Once cooled slightly, roll the doughnuts in the remaining caster sugar.

To serve

Sprinkle a little caster sugar over the brûlée then heat with a blowtorch (or place under a hot grill) until the sugar bubbles and forms a caramel. Arrange the compote and the doughnuts artistically on the plate and we serve ours with raspberry ripple ice cream and fresh raspberries. Enjoy!

The Hart of the Village

The White Hart of Wytham is often described as a hidden gem in the quintessentially English village of Wytham, not far from Oxford, for its freshly prepared food and cosy indoor or summery outdoor dining opportunities.

The White Hart of Wytham has a long history of welcoming guests and wetting whistles, being housed in a 16th century building, and there are records of a pub in the village dating back to 1741, but that was only when the records began! In more recent times, the pub has been under new management since January 2015 and offers more substantial fare to satisfy all appetites.

"We're extremely proud and grateful to have received numerous awards and nominations for our food from The Oxford Times, Bitten Oxford, Ox In A Box and Wadworth Brewery," says Mark Butcher, better known as Baz, the pub's current landlord.

Located a country mile from Oxford city centre, The White Hart is family and dog friendly, boasting two dining rooms, a large bar area, a conservatory, a beautiful secluded courtyard, an outdoor bar, and a renovated Georgian stable turned party room: you'll be spoilt for choice when deciding where to eat or drink and it's lucky that this popular destination also has a very large car park!

In 2020, a number of beautiful gypsy caravan style dining pods were added to the courtyard, so small groups can dine out together under fairy lights in an intimate setting.

Food is always prepared and cooked from scratch on a daily basis at the pub, with the kitchen team – lead by head chef Andrew Carr – using local suppliers wherever possible. You can often find Wytham Woods venison on the menu and there is also a full vegan and vegetarian menu that has garnered its own awards.

The White Hart can cater for all types of events too, whether it's a wedding reception, afternoon tea or birthday party with exclusive hire or group reservations.

Whatever the season or time of year, the pub offers a very hospitable welcome. In the winter there are roaring log open fires and woodburning stoves for extra warmth. In the summer al fresco eating and drinking is hard to beat, amidst the sounds of church bells and swallows, and the appetising aromas from the wood-fired asado barbecue in the courtyard.

Nestled in its lovely village location, The White Hart of Wytham is a place to enjoy award-winning food and drink just a stone's throw from the city in a quiet, unspoilt and historic setting.

Iced Banana Parfait with Salted Caramel

A classic yet simply made pub dessert to round off a great meal, that holds a certain air of elegance and indulgence. This is packed full of flavour, can be enjoyed all year round and is loved by adults and children for its winning combination of banana and salted caramel.

Preparation time: 30 minutes, plus freezing and setting overnight | Serves: 6

For the banana parfait
300ml double cream
2 egg whites
135g caster sugar
250g peeled bananas
10ml lemon juice

For the salted caramel
100g caster sugar
35g unsalted butter
300ml double cream
5g table salt

To garnish
2 bananas
200g salted popcorn

For the banana parfait

Whisk the double cream until it forms soft peaks and slightly holds its shape. Set to one side and in a separate bowl whisk the egg whites until they stiffen up slightly. Add the caster sugar slowly and continue whisking until the whites are smooth, glossy and hold their shape in the bowl. I was once taught as a commis chef that if you can hold this bowl above your head and it does not fall out on you it is ready! Mash the bananas into a smooth pulp and add the lemon juice to stop them going brown. Fold the cream into the banana mix thoroughly and then do the same with the whipped egg whites. Pour into a loaf tin lned with cling film, or you could use teacups or even lollipop moulds as a great cooling treat in the hot weather. Place the parfait in the freezer to set overnight.

For the salted caramel

Dissolve the caster sugar with a splash of cold water in a saucepan over a low heat. Bring to the boil but don't stir at all. When the sugar has turned into a dark golden caramel, whisk in the butter. Remove the pan from the heat and stir in the double cream and salt.

To serve

Slice the parfait and place on top of a pool of salted caramel sauce. Cut the bananas into slices, dust with caster sugar and blow torch them (or place under a hot grill) until caramelised. Add them to the plate and garnish with the popcorn and a scoop of your favourite ice cream. I like to top mine with toffee ice cream but why not try rum and raisin or chocolate: it's up to you!

Hertford Bridge, popularly known as the Bridge of Sighs, Oxford

Directory

Arbequina Restaurant
72-74 Cowley Road
Oxford
OX4 1JB
Telephone: 01865 792777
Email: info@arbequina-oxford.co.uk
Twitter/Instagram/Facebook: @arbequinaoxford

A vibrant, atmospheric, friendly tapas restaurant and bar focused on quality food, wines, sherries and beers.

Aziz @ The Tree
63 Church Way
Iffley Village
Oxford OX4 4EY
Telephone: 01865 775974
Website: aziz.uk.com

Fusing Indian and Bangladeshi cuisines, Aziz Restaurant is a well-established destination in Oxfordshire with a deserved reputation for innovative, creative and delicious food.

Barefoot Oxford
4 Chiltern Business Centre
Garsington Road
Oxford
OX4 6NG
Telephone: 07814495001
Website: www.barefootoxford.co.uk
Email: cake@barefootoxford.co.uk

Artisan bakery, coffee shop and cake lovers' heaven where everything is handmade.

Bhoomi Kitchen
70 London Road
Oxford OX3 7PD
Telephone: 01865 762255
Website: www.bhoomikitchen.co.uk

South Indian restaurant specialising in Indian barbecue, small plates and early bird thali. Indoor, alfresco and takeaway dining.

Cherwell Boathouse
Bardwell Road
Oxford OX2 6ST
Telephone: 01865 552746
Website: www.cherwellboathouse.co.uk
Email: info@cherwellboathouse.co.uk
Facebook and Instagram: @CherwellBoathouse
Twitter: @Cherwell_Boat

A restaurant with a difference, situated on the banks of the River Cherwell close to the centre of Oxford, offering diners the opportunity to experience the true Oxford tradition of punting.

Christine Bakes

Stonecroft
25 Brent Avenue
Didcot
Oxfordshire
OX11 7UD
Telephone: 01235 510168 / 07743 765116
Website: www.christinebakes.co.uk
Facebook: Christine Wallace

Christine demonstrates at food festivals, bakes selected cakes to order, gives baking lessons at home, works with local radio stations, organises the annual food festival in Didcot and much more!

Cuttlefish

37 St. Clements
Oxford OX4 1AB
Telephone: 01865 243003
Email: cuttlefishoxford@gmail.com
Website: www.cuttlefishoxford.co.uk

Seafood restaurant offering an informal yet delicious dining experience that celebrates the bounty of both English and Mediterranean coastlines. Parking available next door in St Clements car park.

Jolly Good Brownies

5 Mill Lane
East Hendred
Oxfordshire
OX12 8JS
Telephone: 07917 542662
Website: www.jollygoodbrownies.co.uk
Instagram: @jollygoodbrownies

Jolly Good Brownies is a mail-order brownie company offering delicious gift wrapped brownies for all occasions.

La Cucina

39-40 St. Clements
Oxford OX4 1AB
Telephone: 01865 793811
Email: lacucinaoxford@hotmail.co.uk
Website: www.lacucinaoxford.co.uk

A family-oriented trattoria and pizzeria with excellent, authentic Italian food at its heart. Parking is available in St. Clements car park next door.

Lotte Duncan

Thame Food Festival
Website: www.thamefoodfestival.co.uk
Twitter: @thamefoodfest
Instagram: @thamefoodfestival
Bradford on Avon Food and Drink Festivals
Website: www.scrumptiousfoodfestivals.co.uk
Twitter: @BoAFoodandDrink
Instagram: @boafoodanddrinkfest

Our aim is to always promote and celebrate fabulous local and national artisan food producers within a fun, vibrant family food festival.

Natural Bread

15/3 Curtis Estate
North Hinksey Lane,
Botley
OX2 0LX
Telephone: 07717 441967
Website: www.naturalbreadcompany.co.uk
Facebook: @naturalbreadox
Twitter: @natural_bread
Instagram: @naturalbread1

Natural Bread is an independent, family-run, Oxford-based artisan bakery, known for handmade sourdough, yeasted breads, pastries and cakes.

No.1 Ship Street
Oxford
OX1 3DA
Telephone: 01865 806637
Website: www.no1shipstreet.co.uk
Social Media: @no1shipstreet

Beautiful modern British brasserie on Ship Street, its namesake, offering top quality produce with a focus on seafood in a great location and vibrant atmosphere.

Nut Tree Inn
Murcott
Main Street
Oxon
OX5 2RE
Telephone: 01865 331 253
Website: www.nuttreeinn.co.uk

Michelin-starred village pub with a warm and friendly atmosphere, cosy indoor spaces and a large garden for drinkers and diners alike.

Oli's Thai
38 Magdalen Rd
Oxford
OX4 1RB
Telephone: 01865 790223
Website: www.olisthai.com

Neighbourhood restaurant with fantastic food that combines the best of European technique and Thai cuisine. Its popularity means booking is highly recommended!

Oxford Fine Dining Ltd
Unit 12, Oddington Grange
Weston on the Green
OXON
OX25 3QW
Telephone: 01865 728240
Email: enquiries@oxfordfinedining.co.uk
Website: www.oxfordfinedining.co.uk
Twitter: @OFDltd
Facebook: @OFDLtd
Instagram: @oxfordfinedining

Catering for weddings, events, dinners and fine dining banquets with innovation and creativity.

Pindy's Samosas Ltd
54 East Field Close
Headington
OX3 7SH
Telephone: 07974 267620 / 07500 650151
Website: pindys.com
Facebook: @pindys.samosas
Instagram: @pindys_samosas

Want delicious savoury or sweet delicacies delivered to your home, event or office? Look no further than Pindy's Samosas for parcelled up perfection.

The Secret Supper Society
Website: www.thesecretsuppersociety.com
Instagram: @secretsupper
Facebook: @TheSecretSupperSociety
Twitter: @thesecretsupper

Self-taught cook Jules hosts a 'home from home' restaurant in the comfortable dining room of her farmhouse in North Oxfordshire, combining restaurant quality food with a relaxed dinner party atmosphere.

Smeg UK
The Magna Building
Wyndyke Furlong
Abingdon
Oxfordshire
OX14 1DZ
Telephone: 0344 557 9907
Website: www.smeguk.com
Email for appointments: showroombooking@smeguk.com

The iconic Italian home appliance manufacturer, headquartered in Abingdon, Oxfordshire.

The Black Horse
81 High Street
Standlake
Oxfordshire OX29 7RH
Telephone: 01865 300307
Email: info@theblackhorsestandlake.com
Website: www.theblackhorsestandlake.com
Instagram: @blackhorse_standlake

Award-winning gastropub with exceptional food and drink and the really friendly welcome that only a true village local can offer.

The Butchers Arms
5 Wilberforce Street
Headington
Oxford
Oxon
OX3 7AN
Telephone: 01865 742470
Email: butchersarmsheadington@gmail.com
Website: butchersarmsheadington.co.uk
Twitter, Facebook and Instagram: butchersarmsox3
Geri, our cat, is also on Twitter: @geripubcat

We're a little tucked-away pub in Headington serving fantastic ales and wines, plus a menu of pub classics and pizzas (full menu on our website).

The Mole Inn
Toot Baldon
Oxford
OX44 9NG
Telephone: 01865 340001
Website: www.themoleinn.com
Email: info@themoleinn.com
Twitter: @The_MoleInn
Instagram: @moleinn
Facebook: @themoleinnoxford

Beautiful 2 AA Rosette country pub and restaurant with a stunning garden, offering fine food, great wines, real ales and relaxed and friendly service.

White Hart
Main Road
Fyfield
Abingdon
Oxfordshire
OX13 5LW
Telephone: 01865 390585
Website: www.whitehart-fyfield.com
Instagram: @thewhitehartfyfield
Twitter: @the_whitehart
Facebook: @whitehartfyfield

Award-winning 15th century dining pub with a passion for fresh seasonal produce and all things local.

The White Hart of Wytham
Wytham
Oxford OX2 8QA
Telephone: 01865 244372
Email: info@whitehartwytham.com
Website: www.whitehartwytham.com
Facebook : @WhiteHartWytham
Instagram:@whitehartofwytham
Twitter: @WhiteHartWytham

Family and dog friendly pub with indoor and outdoor dining and bar areas; a hidden gem in the quintessentially English village of Wytham.

A flower in the tranquillity of the Sobell House garden